SHARE
the
Music

McGRAW-HILL

GRADES K-6

SHARE WORLD MUSIC
SONGS FROM ASIA AND OCEANIA

SERIES AUTHORS

Judy Bond
Coordinating Author
René Boyer-White
Margaret Campbelle-duGard
Marilyn Copeland Davidson
Coordinating Author
Robert de Frece
Mary Goetze
Coordinating Author
Doug Goodkin
Betsy M. Henderson

Michael Jothen
Carol King
Vincent P. Lawrence
Coordinating Author
Nancy L.T. Miller
Ivy Rawlins
Susan Snyder
Coordinating Author

Contributing Writer
Janet McMillion

McGraw-Hill
School Division

New York   Farmington

PROJECT AUTHORS

Margaret Campbelle-Holman
Robert de Frece
Betsy M. Henderson

COORDINATING CONSULTANT

Kathy B. Sorensen

MULTICULTURAL ADVISORS

Cambodian (Khmer)
Jason Roberts
Thida Phon Roberts

Cantonese
Raymond Ho
Elaine Wong

Hebrew
Saul Korewa

Hindi
Chhanda Chakroborti

Hmong
Vilay Her

Japanese
Yoshi Walbeck

Korean
Hong Yong Sohn

Lao / Thai
Tom Toronto

Mandarin
Mei Lee

Maori
David Atkinson

Russian
Elena Budko
Natalia Trusova

Tagalog
Victoria Sohn

Tahitian
Kuinise Matagi
Tearo Matagi

Thai
Thong Sanchez
Gulavadee Vaz

Turkish
Fuat C. Baran

Vietnamese
Le Van Khoa

ACKNOWLEDGMENTS
See page 139.

ILLUSTRATION CREDITS
See page 139.

McGraw-Hill School Division

A Division of The McGraw·Hill Companies

McGraw-Hill School Division
1221 Avenue of the Americas
New York, New York 10020

Printed in the United States of America

ISBN 0-02-295364-7 / K–6

1 2 3 4 5 6 7 8 9 066 02 01 00 99 98

Contents

Introduction

Share World Music is a book of songs and activities intended for use in both multilingual and monolingual classes. Students will become acquainted with a wide range of musical materials encompassing 16 different languages and an array of vocal and instrumental colors.

Share World Music presents songs and listening selections from Asia and Oceania, some selected from the wealth of materials in *Share the Music* and others selected especially for this volume.

- *Songs:* Musical materials include a selection of songs with singable translations. All song pages are reproducible.

- *Lesson Plans:* Complete, easy-to-follow strategies in the **Teaching the Lesson** sections promote musical concept and skill development and encourage exploration of aspects of various cultures. The **Resources** section offers instrumental activities, related arts projects, and movement activities that invite students to work more intensively with the song and to further explore the relevant culture. Technology resources, including *Share the Music* videos and related Web sites, are referenced. Background information provides additional cultural context for the song.

     The lesson plans include two vocabulary-building features: **Vocabulary** words taken from the song for special practice and a **Conversation Corner** that presents greetings and phrases in the language of the song. Printed pronunciation guides are provided for these words and phrases; however, for tonal languages such as Thai, Lao, and Mandarin, these printed guides can only approximate the sounds. Ask students who are native speakers to help pronounce these words and phrases.

- *Visual Aids:* Reproducible song maps allow students to focus on the text and key vocabulary words while they follow the song. Additional visual resources include reproducible flashcards, instrumental parts, and notation from which students can create their own rhythmic patterns.

- *Listening Library:* Listening selections provide additional opportunities to become acquainted with music from the near and far east. Discussion questions and background information are provided for each selection.

- *A Musical Sound Tour:* A narrative explaining the origins and construction of Asian musical instruments is accompanied by recorded examples of the instrumental sounds.

- *Teacher Talk:* This resource section suggests ways that teachers can provide an optimal learning environment for students acquiring English. It also discusses how to best use the lessons and visual aids in the classroom.

- *Classroom Instructions:* Translations and recorded pronunciation guides for important teaching phrases are included in Cambodian (Khmer), Cantonese, Hmong, and Vietnamese.

- *CD Recordings:* All songs are recorded with culturally appropriate instrumentation. Pronunciation guides by native speakers are provided for all non-English lyrics.

Organized to meet diverse teaching needs, *Share World Music* promotes cultural understanding and develops language skills for students of all backgrounds.

CHANG
(Elephant)

Objective
Play instruments with the steady beat and create movement

Materials
Chang (Elephant): Thai/English **CD1:1;**
 Pronunciation **CD1:2**
Visual Aid 1 (Song Map)
unpitched instruments
magazine photograph of elephant (optional)

TEACHING THE LESSON

1. **Introduce the song.** Have students:
   - Close their eyes as you describe an elephant, then guess the animal.
   - Look at **Visual Aid 1** and describe each elephant part. (long nose/trunk, big ears, and so on)
   - Listen as you tell them that they will learn a song naming parts of an elephant.

2. **Teach the song.** Have students:
   - Listen to the song as you point to each elephant part on Visual Aid 1 when it is described in the song. (nguang = trunk, nga = tusk, ta = eye, hu = ear, hang = tail)
   - Show each elephant part by making a body shape. (For example: trunk = arm held out in front of body; ears = spread out hands and extend from head, and so on.)

- Listen again to the song, making their body shapes when you point to each elephant part.
- Repeat the song's name, then listen to it again as they count how many times in a row they hear *chang* at the beginning. (5)
- Count the number of little elephants shown on Visual Aid 1 (5), then listen again to the song, singing *chang* on the same pitch five times in a row at the beginning.
- Learn the Thai words with the recorded pronunciation as you point to the corresponding elephant parts.
- Sing the song as you pat with the beat.

3. **Create movement/assess learning.** Have students:
   - Create an elephant walk using big, slow steps. Step on Beats 1 and 3 in each measure to set the pace.
   - Perform their elephant walk during the musical interludes (when instruments are heard alone without anyone singing).
   - Play unpitched instruments on the steady beat while singing, and do their elephant walk during the interludes.
   - Form two groups, one group singing and playing on the steady beat, the other group doing their elephant walk only during musical interludes. Switch parts.
   - Identify through discussion when they played the steady beat (when they sang along with the recording) and when they showed their elephant walk (during the musical interludes).

RESOURCES

Alternate Activity
Have small groups create an elephant using body shapes. For example, two or three students could form the tusks and trunk.

Art
1. Have students create large pictures of each elephant part. As the song is sung, students can create a "live" Visual Aid by holding up their pictures when each part is named.
2. Invite students to do free-form drawings or paintings of whole

elephants. They may refer to Visual Aid 1 or to photographs.

Math
Ask a librarian for help in finding out the size of an elephant's footprint. Assist students in drawing a life-size elephant footprint on sturdy paper. Then have students stand, one at a time, inside the elephant footprint and trace outlines of their own footprints. Help students count how many of their footprints fit inside the elephant's footprint.

Vocabulary
Refer to Visual Aid 1.

Conversation Corner
สวัสดี ครับ (sa wat˩ di krap˩) = Hello./Goodbye. (said by male)
สวัสดี ค่ะ (sa wat˩ di ka) = Hello./Goodbye. (said by female)
เชิญร้องเพลงกันหน่อย
 (chən rɔng plɛng gʌn nɔi) = Let's sing together.

The phonetics above do not reflect the nuances of this tonal language.

Chang
(Elephant)

Thai Folk Song
Collected and Transcribed by Kathy B. Sorensen

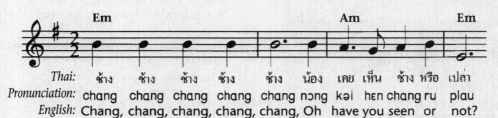

Thai: ช้าง ช้าง ช้าง ช้าง ช้าง น้อง เคย เห็น ช้าง หรือ เปล่า
Pronunciation: chang chang chang chang chang nong kəi hɛn chang ru plau
English: Chang, chang, chang, chang, chang, Oh have you seen or not?

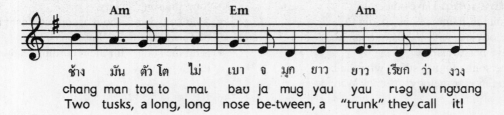

Thai: ช้าง มัน ตัว โต ไม่ เบา จ มูก ยาว ยาว เรียก ว่า งวง
chang man tʋa to maɪ bau ja mug yau yau rɪəg wa ngʋang
Two tusks, a long, long nose be-tween, a "trunk" they call it!

มี เขี้ยว ใต้ งวง เรียก ว่า งา
mik kiu taɪ ngʋang rɪəg wa nga
He has ___ two ___ ears and two eyes, ___

มี หู มี ตา หาง ยาว
mi hu mi ta hang yau
And such a long, long ___ tail.

MALIIT NA GAGAMBA
(Little Spider)

Objective
Perform a finger play while singing a song

Materials
Maliit Na Gagamba (Little Spider): Tagalog/English
CD1:3; Pronunciation **CD1:4**
Visual Aid 2 (Song Map): prepare as a
transparency

TEACHING THE LESSON

1. **Introduce the song.** Have students:
    *   Listen as you tell them they are going to hear a
        familiar melody but with words in a language they
        may not have heard before.
    *   Listen to the song, patting softly with the beat.
    *   Identify the familiar melody. ("Eency Weency
        Spider")

2. **Teach the finger play.** Have students:
    *   Look at **Visual Aid 2** and discuss the story.
    *   Imitate you as you perform each part of the finger
        play. (See **Finger Play,** below.)
    *   Perform the finger play with the recording.

3. **Teach the song/assess learning.** Have
    students:
    *   Listen to and practice the pronunciation for the
        song, using the recorded lesson.
    *   Practice saying the vocabulary words listed. (See
        Vocabulary, below.)
    *   Sing the song slowly.
    *   Sing the song without accompaniment as they
        perform the finger play.
    *   Sing the song with the recording as they perform
        the finger play.

RESOURCES

Finger Play
Measures 1–2: "Walking" motion of
index fingers touching thumbs of
opposite hands. Arms move upward.
Measure 3: Wiggle fingers as arms
move downward.
Measure 4: Sweep arms outward at
waist level.
Measures 5–6: Hands burst open in
front of face to show sun. Continue to
move outward from face through
phrase.
Measure 7: "Walking" motion of
index fingers touching thumbs of
opposite hands. Arms move upward.
Measure 8: "Draw" smile in front of
mouth with both index fingers,
moving them out and up from center.
Measure 9: no finger play

Dramatization
Have students act out the words of the
song. Select one or more students to
portray each role (spider, rain, sun) at
the appropriate points while the class
sings the song.

Playing Instruments
Invite students to play rainsticks on
the second line of the song. Have
them play finger cymbals on the
quarter rests and woodblocks on the
last three notes of the song.

Community Connection
Invite students to ask parents,
grandparents, or neighbors to teach
them other finger play songs to share
with the class. Compare and discuss
with the class any different versions of
songs that are collected.

Vocabulary
gagamba (ga gam ba) = spider
ulan (u lan) = rain
araw (a rau) = sun
masaya (ma sa ya) = happy

Conversation Corner
Kumusta ka? (ku mus **ta** ka) =
    How are you? (greeting among stu-
    dents, teacher to student)
Kumusta po ka yo?
    (ku mus **ta** po ka **yo**) = How
    are you? (student to teacher)
Paalam na. (pa 'a lam na) = Go
    well. (goodbye among students,
    teacher to student)
Paalam po. (pa 'a lam po) = Go
    well. (student to teacher)

Note that some languages such as
Tagalog use a variety of greetings to
indicate levels of respect (older to
younger, for example).

Maliit Na Gagamba
(Little Spider)

Filipino Folk Song
Collected and Transcribed by Miriam B. Factora
English Version by MMH

Tagalog: Ma - li - it na ga-gam-ba u - mak yat sa sa-nga,
Pronunciation: ma li it na ga gam ba u mak yat sa sang a
English: Lit - tle spi-ders climb a branch one bright and sun - ny day,

Du - ma-ting ang u-lan 'Ti - na-boy si-la Su mi kat ang a - raw
du ma ting ang u lan ti na boi si la su mi kat ang a rau
Then the rain comes a-long, wash-es them a-way. Now the sun is shin-ing,

na tu yo ang sa-nga Ma - li-it na ga-gam-ba ay
na tu yo ang sang a ma li it na ga gam ba ai
dry - ing up the rain. Lit - tle spi-ders, climb-ing up are

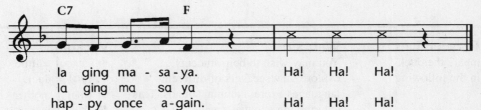

la ging ma - sa - ya. Ha! Ha! Ha!
la ging ma sa ya Ha! Ha! Ha!
hap - py once a-gain. Ha! Ha! Ha!

SHIAU YA
(Little Duck)

Objective
Perform an unpitched percussion accompaniment

Materials
Shiau Ya (Little Duck): Mandarin/English **CD1:5**;
   Pronunciation **CD1:6**
Visual Aid 3 (Song Map)
Visual Aid 4 (Accompaniment Map): prepare as
   transparency
unpitched instruments

TEACHING THE LESSON

1. **Introduce the song.** Have students:
   * Tell what sounds ducks make. (*quack*)
   * Listen as you explain that in Mandarin, the word
     for *quack* is *gwa.*
   * Make a duckbill with their hands and practice
     opening and closing the bill.
   * Listen to the song, opening and closing the duckbill
     each time they hear *gwa.*

2. **Teach the song.** Have students:
   * Follow **Visual Aid 3,** tapping the ducklings in the
     top rows for Measures 1–4 as they respond to the
     short and long *gwa* sounds. For Measures 5–7, have
     students tap the mother duck twelve times with the
     beat, then for Measure 8 tap each little duck once
     with the beat. Do this as they listen to the song
     more than once.
   * Echo the Mandarin words using the recorded
     pronunciation guide.
   * Practice the vocabulary words listed. (See
     Vocabulary, below.)
   * Sing the song with the recording, making the
     duckbill motion each time they sing *gwa.*

3. **Teach an unpitched percussion part/assess
   learning.** Have students:
   * Follow the transparency of **Visual Aid 4,** saying
     swim for each swimming duck and *gwa* for each
     quacking duck. (Each box represents one beat.)
   * Add movement, making a paddling motion with
     their hands as they say *swim* and the duckbill
     motion as they say *gwa.*
   * Perform the movement while thinking the words.
   * Transfer the *gwa* sound to unpitched instruments
     such as a güiro or a mallet scraped over a rough
     surface. (Have students not playing instruments
     continue the paddling and duckbill movements.)
   * Sing the song as some students accompany it with
     the instrumental part and others with the
     movement.

RESOURCES

Multicultural Perspectives
Have students compare the duck
sound as spoken in the following
languages:

English   *quack quack*
Chinese   gwa gwa
French   kwɛ̃ kwɛ̃
Spanish   kwa kwa
Ga (Ghanaian language) kwɔ̃ kwɔ̃
   The *tilde* in the French and Ga
shows that the vowels are pronounced
nasally, like the *n* sound in English.

Web Site
You may wish to help students
explore how speakers of different
languages express animal sounds. This
entertaining site was created by a
linguistics professor and includes
photos and sound effects.
**http://www.georgetown.edu/cball/animals/
animals.html**

Vocabulary
小 (shiau) = little
鴨 (ya) = duck
母 (mu) = mother
快 (kwai) = happy

Conversation Corner
您好。 (nin hao) = Hello.
謝謝。 (shiɛ shiɛ) = Thank you.
再見。 (tsai jiən) = Goodbye.

The phonetics above do not reflect the
nuances of this tonal language.

Shiau Ya
(Little Duck)

Taiwanese Folk Song
Collected and Transcribed by Kathy B. Sorensen
English Version by MMH

Mandarin: 呱 呱 呱 呱 呱 呱 呱
Pronunciation: gwa gwa gwa gwa gwa gwa gwa
English: Gwa gwa __ gwa gwa __ gwa gwa gwa.

呱 呱 呱 呱 呱 呱 呱 游 來 游 去
gwa gwa gwa gwa gwa gwa gwa yu lai yu chü
Gwa gwa _ gwa gwa _ gwa gwa gwa. What a __ song! The __

真 快 活 就 是 母 鴨 帶 小 鴨
jən kwai hwɔ tsiu shi mu ya dai shiau ya
moth - er takes lit - tle duck-lings out to play.

Copyright © 1991 Kathy B. Sorensen

McGraw-Hill School Division

KAERU NO UTA
(Frog's Song)

Objective
Play a rhythm with one, two, and no sound(s) on the beat

Materials
Kaeru No Uta (Frog's Song): Japanese/English **CD1:7;** Pronunciation **CD1:8**
Visual Aid 5 (Song Map): prepare as transparency (optional)
rhythm sticks

TEACHING THE LESSON

1. **Introduce the song.** Have students:
   - Name several animals and imitate the sound of each.
   - Play a game. (Close eyes as you whisper an animal name to a student, who makes the animal's sound for the class to guess.)
   - Listen as you say that today's song shows how Japanese children make frog sounds.

2. **Teach the song.** Have students:
   - Echo as you say *gwa* (gwɑ) and *gero* (ge ɾo), the frog sounds in the song.
   - Pat with the beat as they listen for those words in the song.
   - Listen again, raising hands on hearing *gwa* and wiggling shoulders on *gero*.
   - Look at **Visual Aid 5,** Line 3, as you point out the lily pads, then pat their legs eight times as you touch each lily pad once with the steady beat.

- Repeat patting, saying *gwa* for each frog.
- Discuss what happened to the frog sound on the lily pads without frogs. (silence, no sound, or musical term "rest")
- Identify a beat of silence as a rest.
- Optional: Look at a copy of the printed song and find the rest in Line 1. (𝄽)
- Pat their legs as you touch each lily pad of Line 4 with the beat, then repeat, saying *gero* for each lily pad with two frogs and *gwa* for each lily pad with one frog.
- Listen to the song, patting with the beat and singing Lines 3 and 4. Repeat.
- Echo the recorded pronunciation guide.
- Practice the vocabulary words listed. (See **Vocabulary,** below.)
- Sing the song, following Visual Aid 5, with the recording. Repeat.

3. **Play the rhythm of Lines 3 and 4/assess learning.** Have students:
   - Create a movement that makes no sound. (Examples: stick out "frog" tongue, wink, bob head.)
   - Using rhythm sticks, practice playing one sound with *gwa* and using their soundless movement for the rests in Line 3.
   - Practice making two faster sounds by tapping both rhythm sticks bilaterally on the floor, saying the word *gero* while practicing. Perform Line 4, using their soundless movement for the final rest.
   - Sing the song using the rhythm sticks on Lines 3 and 4 as practiced.

RESOURCES

Alternate Game
Invite students to find where rests go in the song. Looking at Visual Aid 5, ask: "How many rests are needed for Lines 3 and 4?" (5) Have students refer to the printed music to see how many rests are shown in the whole song. (7)

Playing Instruments
Have students name a one-syllable and a two-syllable sound for another animal. (For example, a cat: *purr* and

meow.) Have them sing the song with the new animal name, sounds, and unpitched instruments. (Suggestion: *purr*—güiro; *meow*—tic-toc block.)

Language Arts
Help students compare frog sounds as expressed in Japanese and English. Ask: "What sound do we use in English?" (ribbit) "Would this fit in the song with *gwa* or with *gero*? Why?" (*gero;* has two syllables)

Web Site
For facts, projects, and photos about frogs, visit Frogland.
http://www.teleport.com/~dstroy/index.html

Vocabulary
かえる (kɑ e ɾu) = frog
うたが (u tɑ gɑ) = song

Conversation Corner
こんにちは (kon ni chi wɑ) = Good day.
さよなら (sɑ yo nɑ ɾɑ) = Goodbye.

Kaeru No Uta

(Frog's Song)

Japanese Folk Song
English Version by MMH

do

Japanese: か え る の う た が
Pronunciation: ka e ru no u ta ga
English: **Hear the frog, he sings a song.**

き こ え て く る よ
ki ko e te ku ru yo
It is such a hap - py song:

グワ グワ グワ グワ
gwa gwa gwa gwa
gwa gwa gwa gwa

ゲ ロ ゲ ロ ゲ ロ ゲ ロ グワ グワ グワ
ge ro ge ro ge ro ge ro gwa gwa gwa
ge ro ge ro ge ro ge ro gwa gwa gwa.

SARIKA KAIO
(Myna Birds)

Objective
Move to show groups of beats in ♩

Materials
Sarika Kaio (Myna Birds): Cambodian/English
  CD1:9; Pronunciation **CD1:10**
Visual Aid 6 (Song Map)
color photograph of myna bird (optional)

TEACHING THE LESSON

1. **Introduce the song.** Have students:
   - Name any birds they know that can "talk," or imitate human speech. (parrots, parakeets, myna birds)
   - Discuss whether they have seen any of these birds or where these birds live. (May be seen as pets or in pet shops, zoos, or television documentaries; in the wild, parrots live in tropical Central and South America and Oceania; parakeets in Australia, Southeast Asia, and Africa; and myna birds in India and Southeast Asia.)
   - Look at the myna bird pictured on **Visual Aid 6.**

2. **Teach the song.** Have students:
   - Listen to the song while following Visual Aid 6.
   - Listen to the song again, performing the following pattern with the beat: pat legs, clap hands, snap fingers, clap hands. (Notice the preparatory beats sung before the first full sung measure.)
   - Repeat, being sure to clap very quietly.
   - Learn the Cambodian words with the recorded lesson.

   - Practice saying the vocabulary words listed (see **Vocabulary** below), then listen for them in the song.
   - Echo-sing, then sing the song, following Visual Aid 6.
   - Sing the song again, moving with the beat (pat, clap, snap, clap).

3. **Move to show groups of beats/assess learning.** Have students:
   - Discuss different ways beats can be grouped in music. (twos, threes, fours)
   - Think about the movement they just performed. Decide how many beats were in each group. (4; if students need help, have them perform the movement slowly as they count it. Remind them that the patting always occurs on Beat 1.)
   - Say the following sequence of cue words: Beat 1—*pick*, Beat 2—*eat*, Beat 3—*dancing*, Beat 4—*dancing*.
   - Perform the following movements for each beat while saying cue words. Practice the movement alone first, then with a partner.
     Beat 1—pretend to pick a plum from a tree. (Pick a plum from a different place on the tree each time.)
     Beat 2—place plum in "beak" (mouth).
     Beats 3 and 4—facing partner, either holding hands or with hands on hips, move head forward and backward by pushing neck forward and pulling it back in place.
   - Perform the movement pattern while listening to the song, then while singing the song. On interludes, move to a new partner.

RESOURCES

Alternate Game
Encourage students to create their own four-beat movement pattern for the myna bird's dance. Tell them to include four different movements that are simple enough to do one after the other in time with the music.

Science
Invite students to research and discuss birds that can imitate human speech.

Ask students to find out how these birds learn the words and whether their vocal mechanisms differ from those of birds that do not imitate human sounds.

Vocabulary
សារិកាកែវ (sɑ ɾi k̚a k̚a o) = myna birds
ស្លាប (slɑ) = wings

Conversation Corner
សួស្ដី (sua sədaɪ) = Hello.
អរគុណ (ɔ k̚ɔn) = Thank you.
លាហើយ (lia haʊ i) = Goodbye.

See CD2 for a recorded pronunciation of each phrase.

McGraw-Hill School Division

Sarika Kaio
(Myna Birds)

Cambodian Folk Song
Collected and Transcribed by Kathy B. Sorensen
English Words by Linda Worsley

Cambodian សារិ កា កែវ អើយ ស៊ី អ៊ី កង កង (ហា សា រិ យុង) ស៊ី ផ្លែ ដំ
Pronunciation: saɾi kʰa kʰa əi si əi kʰɔng kʰɔng (haɪ sa ɾi yong) si plaɪ dam
English: Oh, my-na birds, eat-ing plums in the tree, (la la la la), And peck-ing

បង ប្រ ចិក គ្នា លេង អើយ អើយ កែវ
bong pɾɔ jʌkn kniə leng əi əi kʰaɪ o
one an-oth-er____ play-ful-ly. And your

អើយ ស្លាប់ រា ចាក់ ក្បាច់ មាត់ រា ធ្វើ
əi slə viə jak baʔn mɔʔn viə twə
wings____ are danc-ing, mov-ing to the sound, As your

ភ្លេង (ហា សា រិ យុង) ប្រ ចឹក គ្នា លេង ក្នុង ព្រៃ ប្រឹក
plẽng (haɪ sa ɾi yong) pɾɔ jʌk kniə leng kʰɔng pɾeɪ bɾun
beaks, (la la la la), are mak-ing mu-sic all____ a-

សា អើយ អើយ កែវ អើយ
sa əi əi kʰaɪ o əi
round, from high in the tree.

Copyright © 1991 Kathy B. Sorensen

McGraw-Hill School Division

SASARA ANG BULAKLAK
(The Flower Fades)

Objective
Sing and play a game in AB form

Materials
Sasara Ang Bulaklak (The Flower Fades):
    Tagalog/English **CD1:11**; Pronunciation **CD1:12**
Visual Aid 7 (Song Map)

TEACHING THE LESSON

1. **Introduce the song.** Have students:
   - Share any experiences they have had watching plants grow in their homes, gardens, or classrooms. (Ask: How does a leaf or flower look before it opens? Does it open all at once or slowly?)
   - Show with arm movements how a leaf or flower opens. (Ask: How would you show this by yourself, without leaving your seat? How would you show this with a friend? Explain that they will learn a game that shows the movement of a flower opening and closing.)

2. **Teach the song.** Have students:
   - Follow **Visual Aid 7** as they listen to the recording of the song. (Note that a literal English translation is presented beneath the Tagalog; the English text is at the bottom of the page.)

   - Listen again, pointing to the B section on the Visual Aid when they hear *Bum ti ya ya.*
   - On an additional listening, notice that the melody changes and begins to "bounce along" in the B section. Discuss how the steady rhythm of the A section is different from the dotted (uneven) rhythm that occurs in the B section.
   - Listen to the recorded pronunciation guide and echo the words. (This recording also includes game instructions and background.)
   - Practice the vocabulary words listed. (See **Vocabulary** and **Background,** below. If desired, practice both versions of the words.) Then listen again to the song as they find and pronounce the vocabulary words on Visual Aid 7.
   - Sing the song with the recording.

3. **Sing and play the game/assess learning.**
Have students:
   - Form a circle, join hands, and practice the movements of the game. (See **Movement,** below.)
   - Compare the movements used in the A and B sections, listing similarities and differences.
   - Play the game several times while singing the song.
   - Describe in simple terms how each person who was "It" moved during the B section.

RESOURCES

Movement
Formation: circle, holding hands. One student is chosen to be "It."
A Section:
   Measure 1: Move with the quarter note beat. Step forward four steps, raising joined hands over heads (the flower closes).
   Measure 2: Step backward four steps and lower joined hands (the flower opens its petals).
   Measures 3–4: Either stand in place or walk seven steps in one direction around the circle. On the eighth step, all turn and face center and "It" moves into the center in any fancy way.

B Section: "It" continues moving throughout the B section. "It" may choose a new "It" by pointing an exaggerated hip motion to the new "It" on the final *bom*.

Background
In the Tagalog text to this song, an extra syllable has been added to the beginning of some words, possibly to play off the repeated syllable that occurs at the end of *bulaklak.* Thus *sara* (close) becomes *sasara,* *buka* (open) becomes *bubuka,* *ikot* (turn around) becomes *iikot,* and *daan* (way) becomes *dadaan.*

Vocabulary
sara (sa ɾa) = close
buka (bu ka) = open
bulaklak (bu lak lak) = flower

Conversation Corner
Ang pangalan ko ay___.
   (ang pa **nga** lan ko a___) =
   My name is _____.
Kakanta tayo. (ka **kan** ta ta **yo**) =
   Let's sing together.

Sasara Ang Bulaklak
(The Flower Fades)

Filipino Folk Song
English Version by MMH

Tagalog: Sa - sa - ra ang bu - lak - lak,   bu - bu - ka   ang bu - lak - lak,
Pronunciation: sa sa ɾa ang bu lak lak   bu bu ka   ang bu lak lak
English: **In the fall the flow-er fades,**   **In the spring the flow-er blooms,**

I - i - kot ang bu - lak - lak,   Da - da - an ang rey - na.
i i kot ang bu lak lak   da da an ang ɾei na
Now the flow-er turns a-round,   **Make way for the Queen now.**

Bum   ti-ya   ya, bum   ti-ya   ya,   bum   ti-ya   ya ye - ye
bum   ti ya   ya bum   ti ya   ya   bum   ti ya   ya ye   ye
Bum   ti-ya   ya, bum   ti-ya   ya,   bum   ti ya   ya ye - ye

Bum ti-ya ya, bum ti-ya ya, bum ti-ya ya ye - ye   a   bom!
bum ti ya ya bum ti ya ya   bum ti ya ya ye   ye   a   bom
Bum ti-ya ya, bum ti-ya ya,   bum ti ya ya ye - ye   a   bom!

LEK KANSAING
(Hiding the Towel)

Objective
Create a game variation

Materials
Lek Kansaing (Hiding the Towel):
 Cambodian/English **CD1:13**; Pronunciation
 CD1:14
Visual Aid 8 (Song Map)
small towel, handkerchief, or scarf

TEACHING THE LESSON

1. **Introduce the song.** Have students:
   - Tell what kind of games they like to play, both indoors and outside.
   - Name several favorite circle games they know how to play.
   - Tell how music and singing make a game more fun to play. (Singing gives all players something to do as they wait their turn.)

2. **Teach the song.** Have students:
   - Listen to the recording, noticing that a soloist sings once through and a group sings on the repeat each time.
   - Listen again, patting with the beat.
   - Following **Visual Aid 8,** say the rhythm using the rhythm syllables *ta* and *ti*.

- Identify the measure that contains four eighth notes or *ti-ti-ti-ti*. (Measure 3)
- Say the rhythm syllables again while tapping on Visual Aid 8.
- Choose a volunteer to tap and say the syllables alone.
- Listen to and practice the pronunciation of the song.
- Practice saying the vocabulary words. (See **Vocabulary,** below.)
- Sing the song.

3. **Create a game variation/assess learning.**
   Have students:
   - Learn the popular Cambodian circle game played with the song. As the song is sung, "It" walks around the outside of the circle with a knotted dish towel or handkerchief. "It" tosses the towel to a child in the circle. That child gives chase until "It" is caught or is able to take the vacant place in the circle. If "It" gets to the vacant place without being caught, the chaser becomes the new "It."
   - Create a variation of the game to match the theme of the song. (See **Game Variations,** below, for ideas.)

RESOURCES

Game Variations
1. Standing in a circle, students circle to the left during the Cambodian verses and circle to the right on the English verses, squatting down on the last *meow.*
2. Have students sit in a circle with "It" in the center. As students sing the song, they pass the towel behind their backs around the circle. On the last *meow,* all students freeze and "It" guesses who has the towel. "It" may have up to three guesses.

Playing Instruments
Identify the three pitches used in the song (*do re mi*), then play the song on resonator bells or other pitched instruments.

Art
Invite students to make original cat masks out of paper plates to wear as they play the games. The masks can be fastened around students' heads with lengths of yarn.

Multicultural Perspectives
Have students compare this traditional Cambodian game with others they know (for example, "A Tisket A Tasket").

Vocabulary
លាក (lɛk) = hide
កន្សែង (kʼan saɪŋa) = towel
ឆ្មា (chma) = cat

Conversation Corner
សួស្ដី (sua sədaɪ) = Hello.
សុខសប្បាយទេ? (sɔk sa baɪ teɪ) = How are you?
លាហើយ (lia haʊi) = Goodbye.

See CD2 for a recorded pronunciation of each phrase.

McGraw-Hill School Division

Lek Kansaing
(Hiding the Towel)

Cambodian Singing Game
Collected and Transcribed by Kathy B. Sorensen

Cambodian:	លាក់ ក	ខ្សៀង ឆ្មា ខំ	កែង អាស លោង អាស	លោង
Pronunciation:	lɛkˀ kˀan	saɪng chma kam	kˀaɪng o long o	long
English:	**Hide the**	**towel, catch the**	**cat, me - ow, me -**	**ow.**

NABE, NABE, SOKO, NUKE
(Stewpot, Stewpot, Bottomless Pot)

Objective
Follow melodic icons in rhythm with song

Materials
Nabe, Nabe, Soko, Nuke (Stewpot, Stewpot, Bottomless Pot): Japanese/English **CD1:15**; Pronunciation **CD1:16**
Visual Aid 9 (Song Map): prepare as transparency (optional)

TEACHING THE LESSON

1. **Introduce the song.** Have students:
   - List items that could be ingredients in a stew. (vegetables, noodles, meat, broth, seasonings, and so on)
   - Pretend to hold a very small porcelain pot in both hands. Since the pot is full of delicious stew, one must keep it level.
   - Holding the pot in both hands, bounce hands from one leg to the other with the beat while listening to the song. (The first four notes of the introduction set the beat.)
   - Discuss how they follow a path when they travel from their home to a friend's house.
   - Listen as you tell them that they will follow the path a song makes when it is written on a page.

2. **Teach the song.** Have students:
   - Listen to the song, pretending to hold the stewpot and bouncing hands from one leg to the other on the steady beat.
   - Listen again, with eyes closed, imagining following a pathway from their own home to a friend's house.
   - Listen to and practice the pronunciation using the recorded lesson.
   - Learn the vocabulary word listed. (See **Vocabulary,** below.)
   - Sing the song with the recording, bouncing the imaginary stewpot from one leg to the other on the steady beat.

3. **Follow the melodic icons/assess learning.** Have students:
   - Look at **Visual Aid 9** and notice the stewpots.
   - Listen as you tell them that music makes a pathway one can hear, sing, and read. To read a musical pathway, they can follow the printed symbols for what they sing.
   - Sing the song, watching as you touch the stewpots in rhythm. [You may wish to use a transparency of Visual Aid 9; note that the first beat of Line 2 shows the rhythm of the Japanese syllable, not the English. Challenge students to determine whether a whole or divided pot would represent the English words on that beat. (divided)]
   - Touch the stewpots on their own copies of Visual Aid 9 while singing the song again.
   - Describe the "pathway" of the stewpots. (On three different levels; pots move up and down with melody; some are whole and others are divided in two even parts.)

RESOURCES

Game
Have students sit in a circle, with some holding a tennis ball in both hands to represent the stewpot. Move with the beat. Verbal cues: *touch, touch, touch, pass.*
   Beat 1: touch left leg
   Beat 2: touch right leg
   Beat 3: touch left leg
   Beat 4: pass "stewpot" to person on
      right
For a variation, pass only one tennis ball. The student who ends up with the ball on the last rest of the song is out; others continue.

Playing Instruments
Have students write the rhythm pattern of the game above, using *ta* (quarter note) for *touch* and quarter rest for *pass*. They may then play the pattern on unpitched classroom instruments.

Art/Language Arts
Invite students to draw picture maps of their neighborhood, including the path they follow from their home to a friend's house. Have them use directional words, such as forward, straight, turn, left, and right, to describe how to follow the path.

Video Reference
See the *Share the Music* video "Blending Musical Styles" for a clip of Japanese flute playing.

Vocabulary
なべ (na be) = stewpot

Conversation Corner
こんにちは (kon ni chi wa) = Good day.
さよなら (sa yo na ɾa) = Goodbye.

Nabe, Nabe, Soko, Nuke

(Stewpot, Stewpot, Bottomless Pot)

Japanese Singing Game
English Version by MMH

Japanese: な　べ　な　べ　そ　こ　ぬ　け
Pronunciation: na　be　na　be　so　ko　nu　ke
English: **Stew - pot,　stew - pot,　bot-tom-less　pot;**

そ　こ　が　ぬ　け　た　ら　か　え　り　ま　しょ
so　ko　ga　nu　ke　ta　ra　ka　e　ri　ma　sho
Now we turn it　up-side down and　emp-ty out the　pot!

Lesson 9

TANG TANG JUEN
(Round, Round, Turn)

Objective
Perform an instrumental accompaniment

Materials
Tang Tang Juen (Round, Round, Turn):
Cantonese/English **CD1:17**; Pronunciation
CD1:18
Visual Aid 10 (Song Map) (two pages)
Orff instruments

TEACHING THE LESSON

1. **Introduce the song.** Have students:
   - List game songs they know. (Examples: "The Farmer in the Dell," "A la rueda rueda," "London Bridge")
   - Discuss whether all the words to these songs make sense. (No, game songs often have nonsense words.)
   - Listen as you explain that they will learn a Cantonese game song. (See **Game**, below.)

2. **Teach the song.** Have students:
   - Listen to the song, following **Visual Aid 10.**
   - After a second listening, name round or turning things from the song. (flower, rice ball, windmill)
   - Practice echoing the Cantonese words as they listen to the recorded pronunciation.
   - Learn the vocabulary words listed. (See **Vocabulary,** below.)
   - Listen to the song, whispering practiced words.
   - Sing the song with the recording.

3. **Play an accompaniment/assess learning.**
   Have students:
   - Echo you in saying the rhythm of the bass line using the cue words.

   - Pat the rhythm, then transfer it to bass instruments.
   - Sing the song with the bass accompaniment, adding a finger snap on the last beat of each 8-beat phrase.
   - Transfer the snap to soprano and alto glockenspiels.
   - Echo you in saying the rhythm of the temple block part, using the cue words.
   - Learn the changes to all parts for the last measure, played on the final lyric *turn* (of *turn and turn*).

   - Sing the song with the accompaniment.

RESOURCES

Background
This song's imagery evokes the lifestyle of rural Chinese children, some of whom help support their families by raising chickens. Fried rice cakes and sticky rice balls are favored desserts. Annual dragon boat races feature long, colorful boats with fierce dragons' heads and tails, rowed by teams to the beat of a drum.

Game
Playing musical chairs is popular in China. To play, have students hold hands in a circle. Set chairs out behind them, one fewer in number than players. Students circle with the recording; when you unexpectedly stop the recording, they dash for the chairs. The one not seated is out. Repeat, removing a chair each time.

Movement
Have small groups create movement to show the meaning of each phrase.

Art
Help students make pinwheels from an 8" square of lightweight colored paper, a plastic straw, and a thumb tack. Fold paper on both diagonals to crease it. Starting at corners, cut in creases up to one inch from center. Fold each left corner to center. Push tack through all layers and into straw.

Vocabulary
乙 (tang) = round
轉 (juen) = turn
花 (fa) = flower

Conversation Corner
你好。(leɪ ho) = Hello.
謝謝。(tsiɛ tsiɛ) = Thank you.
再見。(jɔɪ gɪng) = Goodbye.

See CD2 for a recorded pronunciation of each phrase.

Tang Tang Juen
(Round, Round, Turn)

Cantonese Folk Song
English Words by Linda Worsley

Cantonese: 丞 丞 轉 菊 花 園
Pronunciation: tang tang juen go' fa yuən
English: **Round, _ round, _ turn; chry - san - the-mum flow'r,**

炒 米 餅 糯 呀 糯 米 團
tsau maɪ beɪn lo a lo maɪ tuən
Rice __ cake __ sweet, ___ stick - y rice to eat.

五 月 初 五 係 龍 舟 節 呀
m yʊ chɔ m haɪ lon tsau tsi a
May the fifth is the day of the dra-gon boats.

阿 媽 佢 叫 我 去 睇 龍 船
a ma kɔɪ giu o ɔɪ hɔɪ taɪ lon shən
Moth-er says, "Go and see, Go see the dra-gon boats."

我 唔 去 睇 我 要 去 睇 雞 仔
o m hɔɪ taɪ o yu hɔɪ taɪ gaɪ tsaɪ
"No, I would rath-er watch my lit - tle bab - y chick-ens!"

雞 仔　　大 我 叻 去 賣
gaɪ tsaɪ　　daɪ o le hɔɪ maɪ

When they're grown I'll take　them, take ___ them to sell.

賣 得 幾 多 錢
maɪ dʌ geɪ do tsin

How　much mon - ey will I make　there?

賣 咗 幾 多 隻 呀 我
maɪ jɔ geɪ do tsaɪ a o

How　man - y chick-ens should I take there?　I

有 隻 風 車 仔 佢 轉 得 好 好
yau tsaɪ fong chɛɪ tsaɪ kɔɪ chun dʌ ho ho

have _ a lit - tle _ wind-mill. _ When it turns, it's beau-ti-ful to

睇　　　睇 佢 乑 乑 轉
taɪ　　　taɪ kɔɪ tang tang juen

see! _____ See it round, _ round, _ turn;　chry -

菊　花　園　睇　佢　丞　丞　轉　呀
go' fa yuən taɪ kɔɪ tang tang juən a
san - the-mum flow'r. See it round, _ round, _ turn, a -

To Coda ⊕   *ad lib*   *D.S., last time al Coda* ⊕ *Coda*

丞　丞　轉　又　轉　睇　佢　轉
tang tang juən ya juən taɪ kɔɪ juən
round, _ round, _ turn, and turn, See it turn.

CHUỘT CẮP TRÚ'NG
(The Mouse and the Egg)

Objective
Dramatize a folk song

Materials
Chuột Cắp Trú'ng (The Mouse and the Egg):
    Vietnamese/English **CD1:19**; Pronunciation
    CD1:20
Visual Aid 11 (Song Map)
large beach ball or pillow

TEACHING THE LESSON

1. **Introduce the song.** Have students:
    - Imagine that they have to move a heavy object such as a trunk but can't move it alone. Determine how a friend might be able to help them move it.
    - Give suggestions as to how a mouse could help another mouse move an object such as a large egg.
    - Pick volunteer "actors" to pretend they are lifting a heavy object alone without success, using a pillow or beach ball as a prop.

2. **Teach the song.** Have students:
    - Listen to the song, following **Visual Aid 11.**
    - Discuss the story, determining which mouse is smarter, the thief or the friend who is summoned to help. Explain their choice.
    - Look at the song to find the measures containing the nonsense syllables. (Measures 13, 15)

- Determine which measures begin with two C quarter notes (third space C) and which of those measures are the same. (Measures 1, 3, 5, 7; Measures 1 and 5 are the same; Measures 3 and 7 are the same.)
- Use the recorded lesson to practice the pronunciation for the song.
- Practice saying the vocabulary words listed. (See **Vocabulary,** below.)
- Echo-sing, then sing the song, following Visual Aid 11.

3. **Dramatize the song/assess learning.** Have students:
    - Use Visual Aid 11 to review the events of the story by cutting the four pictures apart, mixing up the pieces, and putting them in the correct order.
    - Select two volunteers to dramatize the events as the group sings the song. The actors take their cues from this synopsis:
        Measures 1–4: A mouse finds an egg and can't carry it alone.
        Measures 5–6: The mouse calls another mouse to help.
        Measures 7–8: The second mouse forms a plan to move the egg.
        Measures 9–16: The mice carry out the plan as described by the song lyrics.
    - Choose other pairs of volunteers to act out the story as time permits.

RESOURCES

Background
The Vietnamese language includes many words from Chinese, Thai, and other Asian languages. Historically, the writing system used ideograms, or symbols that stand for ideas, as is still the case in the Chinese language. In the 1600s, however, European missionaries created a writing system for the Vietnamese using Roman-style letters, and that system is the one more commonly used now.

Art
Make paper-plate masks with paper ears and yarn whiskers to wear during the dramatization.

Language Arts/Drama
1. Create and dramatize alternate endings to this story.
2. Dramatize the story with original dialogue instead of singing. Have the group make appropriate sound effects to enhance the story.

Vocabulary
chú (chu) = little
chuột (chuət) = mouse
trứng (chung) = egg

Conversation Corner
Chào. (chao) = Hello.
Cám ơn. (kam ən) = Thank you.
Xin chào. (sin chao) = Goodbye.

See CD2 for a recorded pronunciation of each phrase.

Chuột Cắp Trứng
(The Mouse and the Egg)

Vietnamese Folk Song
Collected and Transcribed by Kathy B. Sorensen
English Words by Linda Worsley

Vietnamese: Chú chuột cắp trứng ra không biết làm sao kéo đi, liền gọi
Pronunciation: chu chuɔt kap chɯng ɾa xɔng biɛt lam saʊ kɛo di liɛn gɔi
English: **Lit - tle Mouse went out and found an egg to steal, But he**

chú khác ra, chú kia bày mưu khó gì. Anh nằm
chu xak ɾa chu kia baɪ mu xɔ zi aɪn nam
could - n't lift it, so he had to squeal: "Lit - tle

ngửa bốn chân anh cố mà ôm trứng đi. Tôi thì
ngʊə bon chɑn aɪn kʼo ma om chɯng di tʼɔɪ ti
friend, it's heav - y! Can you help me now?" Said his

nằm cái đuôi kéo anh về hang tức thì.
nam kaɪ dɔɪ kɛo aɪn ve hang tʼʊk ti
mouse friend, "Hold the egg, I'll show you how:

McGraw-Hill School Division

CHUỘT CẮP TRÚ'NG (The Mouse and the Egg) PAGE 2

Một chú ôm trứng nằm vảnh cái đuôi lên trời.
mɔt chu om chʊng nạm vaɪn kaɪ dɔɪ lɛn chɔɪ
Lie up - on your back, Give your tail to me,

Chú kia dơ cái mồm. Kéo cái đuôi, kéo dài.
chu kia zə kaɪ mom kɛo kaɪ dɔɪ kɛo zaɪ
Pull - ing with my teeth, I will drag you free!"

Hò dô dô. Nào dô lên.
hɔ zo zo naɔ zo len
Ho ho hum! Hard - er, now!

Hò dô dô, á!
hɔ zo zo a
Ho ho hum! Ow!

DETA, DETA
(The Moon)

Objective
Show phrase length with movement

Materials
Deta, Deta (The Moon): Japanese/English **CD1:21**;
   Pronunciation **CD1:22**
Visual Aid 12 (Song Map): prepare as transparency
(optional)

TEACHING THE LESSON

1. **Introduce the song.** Have students:
    *   Agree that when one reads a book, one follows the words to understand the story.
    *   Discuss what they follow when they sing a song. (Have them think about what they hear, see, and feel. Possible answers: melody heard, ideas in text.)

2. **Teach the song.** Have students:
    *   Say *moon* as they gently pat both legs simultaneously. Then say *shining* as they pat their legs alternately.

    moon moon moon moon   shin-ing shin-ing shin-ing shin-ing

    *   Follow the moon icons on **Visual Aid 12** while saying and patting *moon* and *shining*. Place one finger silently on their lips for each rest. (Large moon icon = *moon*; small pairs of moons = *shining*).
    *   Perform the above movement and speech quietly while listening to the song. Repeat.

*   Discuss whether they were following the song's pitch or rhythm. (Rhythm; rhythm determines how long or short each sound is while pitch places sound higher or lower.)
*   Listen to and practice the pronunciation of the words using the recorded lesson.
*   Practice the vocabulary words listed. (See **Vocabulary,** below.)
*   Sing the song with the recording, following Visual Aid 12.

3. **Teach the movement/assess learning.** Have students:
    *   Trace the curved lines on Visual Aid 12 with their finger as they sing "Deta, Deta." (You may wish to use a transparency of Visual Aid 12.)
    *   Discover that the lines show the song's phrases.
    *   Define how song phrases are like sentences of a story. (Like sentences, musical phrases communicate ideas that the composer wants us to hear and feel.)
    *   Pretend to hold a large round tray in their hands. Listen to the song, moving the imaginary tray from the left side of the body, over the head, to the right side of the body. (This simulates the arch of the curved lines on Visual Aid 12.) The movement should be slow and last as long as an entire phrase.
    *   When the next phrase begins, pick up a new "tray" from the left side and repeat the movement. (This reinforces reading from left to right.)
    *   Determine how many phrases there are. (3)
    *   Repeat the movement while singing the song.
    *   Sing the song again, performing the movement or tracing the lines on Visual Aid 12.

RESOURCES

Playing Instruments
Have students use the icons on Visual Aid 12. Play *moon* on an instrument that uses one hand, such as a hand drum or woodblock. Play *shining* on an instrument that uses two hands, such as temple blocks or a log drum. Play no sound on the rests.

Once students thoroughly understand the concept of quarter rest, they may play a triangle very softly on the rests instead of playing no sound.

Sing the Japanese verse, playing only the triangle on each rest. For the

first English verse, play all instrument parts above. For the second English verse, sing and play the triangle.

Music Reading
Have students discuss ways to follow music in addition to using rhythm and phrases. Help them realize they can follow, or "read," either the printed words or the notes. Have them follow the lyrics and notes on the printed music, separately at first, then together, while listening to the song.

Vocabulary
つき (tsu ki) = moon
まるい (ma ru i) = round

Conversation Corner
こんにちは (kon ni chi wa) = Good day.
いっしょにうたいましょう (i sho ni u ta i ma sho) = Let's sing together.
さよなら (sa yo na ra) = Goodbye.

Deta, Deta
(The Moon)

Japanese
Children's Song
Collected and Transcribed by
Kathy B. Sorensen

2. Now the moon is hiding!
    Gone away, O gone away,
    Behind the clouds.
    Black as ink, behind the clouds.

WANG Ü GER
(Chinese Fishing Song)

Objective
Identify and accompany phrases of a song

Materials
Wang Ü Ger (Chinese Fishing Song):
   Mandarin/English **CD1:23**; Pronunciation
   CD1:24
Visual Aid 13 (Song Map)
Visual Aid 14 (Fishy Flash Cards)
classroom percussion instruments

TEACHING THE LESSON

1. **Introduce the song.** Have students:
   - Raise a hand if they have ridden in a boat propelled only by oars.
   - Demonstrate how one might row to get someplace fast, then how to row to avoid frightening fish they want to catch.

2. **Teach the song.** Have students:
   - Listen to "Wang Ü Ger," following **Visual Aid 13** and counting the number of phrases in the song.
   - Listen again, demonstrating the length of each phrase by throwing out imaginary fishing nets at the start of each phrase and lowering arms by the end of each phrase.
   - Find three notes together that are the same pitch, then tell which phrase does not end with three identical pitches.

- Locate the measure that contains a wide leap. (Measure 9: low *do* to high *do*)
- Listen to and practice the pronunciation of the song, following Visual Aid 13.
- Practice saying the vocabulary words. (See **Vocabulary,** below.) You may also want to point out on the song page the characters that stand for the vocabulary words.
- Sing the song, showing each phrase by making an arc in the air, moving from left to right.

3. **Teach instrumental accompaniments/assess learning.** Have students:
   - Listen to the song and tap two fingers in the palm on the first beat of every third measure in a phrase.

   Pattern 1

   - Listen again, lightly clapping each of the last three notes in each phrase.

   Pattern 2

   - Divide into two groups, each performing one of the patterns as they sing, then switch parts.
   - Choose volunteers to play Pattern 1 on a gong or cymbal and others to play Pattern 2 on temple blocks or woodblocks.
   - Divide the class into four groups; each group sings one phrase to tell the story.

RESOURCES

Playing Instruments
Starting with Middle C, have students build the C pentatonic scale with resonator bells.

   Have volunteers play the last three notes of each phrase on melody bells as the class sings the song.

Flash Cards
Prepare flash cards from **Visual Aid 14.** Have students match a flash card with each start and end of a phrase. Ask them to tell which card shows

the ending of the song and why. (double bar)

Art
1. Have students design original fish of bright colors. They should make two sides for each fish, add stuffing of crumpled newsprint, then staple the edges together.
2. If possible, find pictures of traditional carp kites and learn to construct one.

Vocabulary
浪 (lang) = wave
網 (wang) = net
魚 (yü) = fish

Conversation Corner
您好。(nin hao) = Hello.
大家一起唱。(da jar i chi tsɔng)
   = Let's sing together.
再見。(tsai jiən) = Goodbye.

The phonetics above do not reflect the nuances of this tonal language.

Wang Ü Ger

(Chinese Fishing Song)

Chinese Folk Song
Collected and Transcribed
by Kathy B. Sorensen
English Version by MMH

Mandarin: 白　淚　滔　滔　我　不　怕
Pronunciation: bai　lang　tau　tau　wɔ　bu　pa
English: Though the waves ___ run ___ high and deep,

掌　穩　舵　兒　往　前　划
jang　wɛn　duɔ　ər　wang　chiɛn　hwa
We sail on ___ the ___ course we keep.

撒　網　下　水　到　魚　家
sa　wang　sia　shue　dau　yü　jia
Throw the net ___ and ___ let it fall,

捕　條　大　魚　笑　哈　哈
bu　tiau　da　yü　siau　ha　ha
Catch the big - gest ___ fish of all.

TITITOREA
(Maori Stick Game)

Objective
Sing, conduct, and play a stick game in $\frac{3}{4}$

Materials
Tititorea (Maori Stick Game): **CD1:25;**
  Pronunciation **CD1:26**
Visual Aid 15 (Song Map)
two paper bags or 1 1/2" diameter tubes per
  student (see **Making Maori Sticks,** in
  Resources)

TEACHING THE LESSON

1. **Introduce the song.** Have students:
   - Explore $\frac{3}{4}$ meter by imitating you as you show the two patterns below:

     Pattern 1   *pat*   *clap*   *snap*
     Pattern 2   *stamp*   *snap R*   *snap L*

   - Conduct in $\frac{3}{4}$ while counting each beat.
   - Work in pairs to create their own body percussion or movement showing $\frac{3}{4}$.

2. **Teach the song.** Have students:
   - Listen to the song, following **Visual Aid 15.**
   - Show the meter in one of the ways just practiced while listening to the song again, counting softly with the beat.
   - Learn the Maori words.
   - Sing the song with the recording.

3. **Play the game/assess learning.** Have students:
   - Form groups of three and learn a stick game. Two students play as the third says the cue words on the song map. Switch roles. (Tell students to hold sticks vertically, not tipped out or pointed at others.)

     floor   tap   out

   - Identify the meter of the stick game. (triple)
   - Sing the song with the recording as they play the stick game. Two students in each group play and the third conducts in three.
   - Switch roles within their groups.

RESOURCES

Stick Game Variations
1. Challenge groups to use a new pattern for Lines 2–3 (*E papa...*) each time through the song.
   Lines 1, 4–5: Always return to original *Floor-Tap-Out* pattern
   Lines 2–3, first time: *Floor-Tap-Right* (repeat pattern 8 times, clicking right sticks together on Beat 3)
   Lines 2–3, second time: *Floor-Tap-Left* (click left sticks)
   Lines 2–3, third time: *Floor-Tap-Both* (click both sticks together, being careful of partner's knuckles)
2. In the Maori version, partners toss sticks to each other, catching them with the newly empty hand, on each third beat of the new patterns above. If appropriate, invite partners to carefully toss and catch right, left, or both sticks in rhythm instead of clicking them. Tossing the sticks up

in a slight arch aids in catching. Help students decide whose sticks will travel to the inside when tossing both sticks. Remind them to keep the sticks vertical.

Making Maori Sticks
Cut PVC pipe 1 1/2" in diameter and 12"–16" long or roll up a large paper bag for each stick. Students can reinforce and decorate the pipes or bags at both ends using tape in Maori colors of red, white, and black.

Background
Maori players, sometimes in rows or circles, deftly throw and catch sticks up to three feet long. Some think that traditionally the sticks were to touch mid-throw, creating a pitched tone. Others think that players skillfully avoided touching sticks.

Vocabulary
The ancient words to "Tititorea" literally tell how sad *Rangi,* the sky, is to be apart from *Papa,* the earth. Maori people no longer associate the meanings with the words when enjoying this song.

Conversation Corner
Kia ora. (ki a **o** ɾa) = Hello.
E waiata tatou.
  (e **waı** a ta ta **toʊ**) = Let's sing together.
E noho ra. (ɛ no ho ɾa) = Goodbye. (said to one staying)
Haere ra. (**ha** e ɾe ɾa) = Goodbye. (said to one going)
Ta. (ta) = Thank you.

Tititorea
(Maori Stick Game)

New Zealand Folk Song
Collected and Transcribed
by Kathy B. Sorensen

Copyright © 1991 Kathy B. Sorensen

HAG SHAVUOT
(Festival of First Fruits)

Objective
Notate the rhythm of a song in 4/4 meter using
♫ , ♩ , 𝄽 , and 𝅗𝅥

Materials
Hag Shavuot (Festival of First Fruits):
  Hebrew/English **CD1:27**; Pronunciation **CD1:28**
Visual Aid 16 (Song Map)
Visual Aid 38 (Rhythmic Building Blocks)

TEACHING THE LESSON

1. **Introduce the song.** Have students:
   - Name some things for which they are thankful and list times of the year when we think about giving thanks. (Thanksgiving, birthdays, other special times)
   - Look at **Visual Aid 16** and locate the song title, "Hag Shavuot." (Explain that the title literally means "holiday weeks." This holiday falls seven weeks after Passover and celebrates the first fruits of the spring harvest. Farmers of ancient Israel brought the first fruits to Jerusalem to give thanks.)

2. **Teach the song.** Have students:
   - Listen to the song, following Visual Aid 16.
   - Sing the melody with the recording, using the syllable *la*.
   - Echo the Hebrew words, using the recorded pronunciation guide.
   - Practice the vocabulary words listed. (See **Vocabulary,** below.)
   - Looking at Visual Aid 16, practice saying the Hebrew words. (Explain that the translation under each picture gives the literal meaning of the Hebrew words.)
   - Sing the song with the recording.

3. **Notate the rhythm of the song/assess learning.** Have students:
   - Work in pairs to cut out the rhythmic building blocks from **Visual Aid 38.**
   - Use the building blocks to notate the rhythm of the song in the open boxes.
   - Sing the song and evaluate the accuracy of their notation.

RESOURCES

Movement
Formation: circle, facing counterclockwise
A Section:

  right   bend   together   bend

Step right foot to the right, bend both knees, place left foot next to right, bend knees. Quickly turn to face clockwise, repeat steps, then turn to face counterclockwise. Repeat A section, but at the end turn to face the center of the circle.
B Section:

  left   bend   together   bend

While raising arms, step left foot forward into circle, bend knees, place right foot next to left, bend knees. Repeat steps, backing out of circle and bringing arms down. Repeat B section.

Reading Hebrew
Hebrew reading order is from right to left, but in music notation it is reversed. Visual Aid 16 shows the Hebrew characters in reading order. However, the Hebrew words are arranged from left to right to go with the English translation underneath.

Language Arts
Have students use Visual Aid 16 to compare the literal English translation with the English song text. Ask students to sing the literal translation with the melody. They will find that the accents of the words fit the music very awkwardly. Discuss how a translator solved this problem.

(created new phrases, reworded English text so it fit song rhythm)

Video Reference
See the *Share the Music* video "Music and Movement" for a clip of Israeli line dancing.

Web Site
For more on Shavuot, see this site:
http://www.holidays.net/shavuot/

Vocabulary
פְּרָחִים (pra **xim**) = flowers
בִּכּוּרִים (bi ku **rim**) = first fruits

Conversation Corner
שָׁלוֹם (sha **lom**) = Hello./Goodbye.
שְׁמִי____ (shmi___) = My name is____.
תּוֹדָה (to **da**) = Thank you.

Hag Shavuot
(Festival of First Fruits)

Traditional Israeli
Holiday Song
English Version by MMH

Hebrew: חַג שָׁ - בוּ - עוֹת, חַג שָׁ - בוּ - עוֹת, חַג שָׁ - בוּ - עוֹת הַ -
Pronunciation: xag sha vu ot, xag sha vu ot, xag sha vu ot hi
English: **Hag Sha-vu-ot,** *hag sha-vu-ot,* *hag sha-vu-ot* the __

בָּא זֶה נֶה. עַל רָא - שִׁי - נוּ זֵר - פְּרָ - חִים
ne ze ba. al ɔʃ she nu zer prɑ xim
fruit is here. **We shall dress our** **hair with gar - lands**

בְּ - יָ - דֵי - נוּ בִּ - כּוּ - רִים. בִּ - כּוּ - רִים.
bə ya de nu bi ku rim bi ku rim
car - ry first fruits __ **in our hands.** **in our hands.**

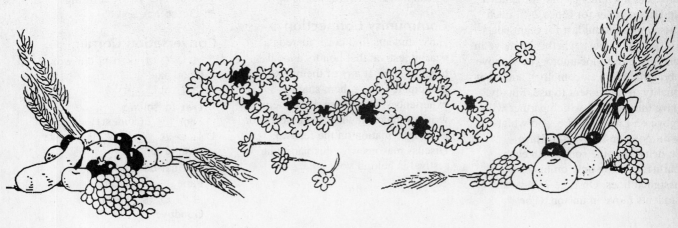

SAKURA
(Cherry Blossoms)

Objective
Identify same and different rhythms

Materials
Sakura (Cherry Blossoms): Japanese/English
  CD1:29; Pronunciation **CD1:30**
Visual Aid 17 (Song Map)

TEACHING THE LESSON

1. **Introduce the song.** Have students:
   - Name some neighborhood plants or flowers that they look for when spring comes. (leaves on trees, daffodils, tulips, cherry, apple, or pear blossoms)
   - Describe other changes that occur in the spring. (Bears leave hibernation, people shed heavy coats and scarves, robins and other birds return to colder climates.)
   - Listen as you tell them that the Japanese word *sakura* means "cherry blossoms" and that the song "Sakura" is about springtime.

2. **Teach the song.** Have students:
   - Listen to the song, touching the beat bars on **Visual Aid 17.**
   - Listen again, this time tracing the shape of the melody in the air with one hand.
   - Learn the Japanese words using the recorded pronunciation guide, following Visual Aid 17. Repeat as needed.
   - Practice the vocabulary words listed. (See **Vocabulary**, below.)
   - Sing the song, following Visual Aid 17.

3. **Identify same and different rhythms/ assess learning.** Have students:
   - Follow the beat bars and sing the song again to determine if the rhythm heard in Line 1 is repeated anywhere in the song. (Line 6–both rhythm and melody are the same.) (Have students circle both lines on Visual Aid 17.)
   - Sing the song again to see if the rhythm of Line 2 is repeated anywhere.
   - Discover that Lines 2, 3, 4, and 5 all have the same rhythm. If students need help, ask them to notice which lines begin with four equal sounds, one with each of the first four beat bars (four quarter notes). (Have students draw rectangles around these lines.)
   - Determine that Line 7 has no rhythmic match.
   - Divide into two groups, one group singing only the lines that are circled and the other sing only those lines in rectangles. Have both groups sing Line 7.

RESOURCES

Movement
In pairs, have students create two different movements, one for Lines 1 and 6, the other for Lines 2–5. Each movement should last for eight beats. Have them choose whether to move in one place (non-locomotor) or to move about the room (locomotor), and what quality of movement to use. Finally, have them decide which partner will move on Lines 1 and 6, and which will move on Lines 2–5. Have students sing the song, with each partner moving only on his or her assigned lines. On Line 7, have all students move in unison. (For example, beckon with right hand for four beats, repeat with left hand, then spread hands outward, palms up.)

Community Connection
Have students find out if there is a nearby festival that honors a local plant or crop. If any of them have participated, have them share experiences. Otherwise, have them write to the chamber of commerce for more information on the festival. Discuss reasons why this particular festival is held in your area.

Vocabulary
さくら (sa ku ɾa) = cherry blossoms
やよい (ya yo i) = spring
そら (so ɾa) = sky

Conversation Corner
こんにちは (kon ni chi wa) = Good day.
わたしは____です
  (wa ta shi wa ____ de su) = I am ____. (student)
わたしは____せんせいです
  (wa ta shi wa ____ sen sei de su) = I am ____. (teacher)
さよなら (sa yo na ɾa) = Goodbye.

Sakura
(Cherry Blossoms)

Japanese Folk Song
English Version by MMH

Japanese: さくら　さくら　やよいの　そらは
Pronunciation: sa ku ɾa　sa ku ɾa　ya yo i no　so ɾa wa
English: **Cher-ry tree,　Cher-ry tree!　Cher-ry blos-soms　ev'-ry-where.**

みわたす　かぎり　かすみか　くもか
mi wa ta su　ka gi ɾi　ka su mi ka　ku mo ka
Far as an-y　eye can _see.　Mist and beau-ty　fill the _ air,

におい ぞ　い ず る　いざや　いざや
ni o i zo　i zu ɾu　i za ya　i za ya
Love-ly blos-soms　scent the _breeze. Come with me,　come with me,

み　に　ゆ　か　ん
mi　ni　yu　ka　n
Let ___ us　go ___ and　see.

TAI YAU TSAI
(Herding the Cows)

Objective
Play ostinatos on unpitched instruments

Materials
Tai Yau Tsai (Herding the Cows):
  Cantonese/English **CD1:31;** Pronunciation
  CD1:32
Visual Aid 18 (Song Map)
Visual Aid 19 (Ostinatos)
unpitched instruments (cymbal, drum, triangle,
  woodblock)

TEACHING THE LESSON

1. **Introduce the song.** Have students:
   - List animals that they have had experience caring
     for, whether at home or elsewhere.
   - Name some animals that make suitable pets at
     home and others that do not.
   - Discuss why a cow is not a good house pet. Suggest
     characteristics such as size, habitat, and needs.

2. **Teach the song.** Have students:
   - Listen to the song, following **Visual Aid 18,** to
     discover what job the singer does. (herds cows)
   - Listen again, patting with the steady beat on the left
     knee while patting eighth notes on the right knee.
     (First practice each hand separately, as needed.)
   - Look at the music to find the measure with the
     octave interval. (Measure 16, C to C')

   - Listen to the song again to determine how many
     measures have the same melody. (Measures 1–4
     and 11–14)
   - Listen to and practice the pronunciation for the
     song using the recorded lesson.
   - Practice saying the vocabulary words listed. (See
     Vocabulary, below.)
   - Echo-sing, then sing the song, following Visual
     Aid 18.

3. **Teach the ostinatos/assess learning.** Have
   students:
   - Use **Visual Aid 19** to learn and practice each
     ostinato, first by clapping or tapping, then by
     playing unpitched instruments.
   - Say the cue words with each ostinato as an aid to
     learning the patterns.
   - Divide into four groups to practice and perform
     each ostinato, rotating until all groups have
     practiced all patterns.
   - Sing the song as a small group of instrumentalists
     plays the ostinatos in succession, repeating each
     one for a total of four measures before playing the
     next. (Tell them not to play on the interlude.)
   - Designate one ostinato for each of the four larger
     groups, each of which then plays its ostinato during
     the two-measure interlude between verses.
   - Select soloists to perform chosen patterns as the
     class sings, using two measures of one ostinato as
     an introduction.

RESOURCES

Background
While Mandarin is the most common
dialect and the official language of
China, there are a number of other
major dialects, including Cantonese.
All of the dialects use the same
written characters, but pronunciations,
vocabulary, and grammar vary so
widely that people speaking one
dialect may not understand those
speaking another.

Student Conductor
Have a student conductor randomly
cue in and cut off groups of ostinato
players.

Body Percussion
Have students clap the woodblock
pattern, snap the triangle pattern, pat
the cymbal pattern, and stamp the
drum pattern.

Rhythm Syllables
Have students figure out the rhythm
syllables of each ostinato and speak
them as they play.

Vocabulary
睇 (tai) = herding
牛 (yau) = cow
山 (san) = hill

Conversation Corner
你 好。(lei ho) = Hello.
你 好 嗎? (lei ho ma) = How are
  you?
下 次 再 見。(ha tsi joi gung) = See
  you next time.

See CD2 for a recorded pronunciation
of each phrase.

Tai Yau Tsai
(Herding the Cows)

Cantonese Folk Song
English Words by Linda Worsley

Cantonese: 睇 牛 仔 技 藝 多
Pronunciation: tai yau tsai gei yai dɔ
English: **Herd - ing the cows _____ takes much __ skill.**

一 口 氣 爬 到 上 山 坡
yʌ hau hei pa do sʌn san bo
Tak - ing a breath, I climb up the hill.

看 守 牛 羊 本 領 大
hɔn sau yau yən bun leng daɪ
Watch - ing cows, what skill it ____ takes!

木 笛 呢 吹 奏 更 柔 揚
mɔ daɪ lei chɔi tsau gʌng yau yʌn
I play my flute, __ Hear the sound it ____ makes.

(Instrumental interlude)

睇 牛 仔　　技 藝 多
tai yɑʊ tsai　　gei yɑi dɔ
Herd - ing the cows ——————— takes much — skill.

一 口 氣　　爬 到 上 山 坡 看
yʌ hɑʊ heɪ　　pa dɔ sʌn san bo han
Tak - ing a breath, I climb up the hill. I

山 坡 青 青　　草 原 長 看
san bo tsɛng tsɛng　　cho yun chʌn han
see green — hills, the — mea - dow long, I

牛 兒 羊 兒 健 又　　強
yɑʊ yi yən yi ging yɑu　　kə
see my cows are health - y and strong.

HOE ANA TE VAKA
(Paddle the Canoe)

Objective
Perform a group movement

Materials
Hoe Ana Te Vaka (Paddle the Canoe):
  Tahitian/English **CD1:33;** Pronunciation **CD1:34**
Visual Aid 20 (Song Map): prepare as two
  transparencies
Visual Aid 38 (Rhythmic Building Blocks)
large woodblocks, slit drums, or log drums

TEACHING THE LESSON

1. **Introduce the song.** Have students:
    *   Discuss any experiences they may have had riding
        in a rowboat, kayak, or canoe. (Point out that in a
        small boat it is important to row steadily and evenly
        so that the boat will keep moving forward.)
    *   Listen as you explain that they will learn a canoe
        song sung in Tahiti for many years.
    *   Paddle twice per measure (on each half note) as they
        listen to the song. (Explain that this song is called an
        'aparima and the movement that goes with it is as
        important as the song words; the movement is
        always performed when the song is sung.)

2. **Teach the movement and the song.** Have
    students:
    *   Kneel in canoe formation.

*   Look at the movements shown on **Visual Aid 20**
    and say the words below the notation in rhythm.
    (The art on the Visual Aid is drawn so that
    mirroring it will produce the correct movements.)
*   Mirror the movements shown in the pictures three
    times through, first saying, then whispering, and
    finally thinking the movement words. (Song form is
    ABA.)
*   Practice performing the movement with the song
    recording several times. (Explain to students that
    pointing up and down on *Tahiti* and *Mo'orea* shows
    the relative locations of Tahiti and Mo'orea, two
    South Pacific Islands.)
*   Listen to the recorded pronunciation guide and
    practice the Tahitian words.
*   Practice the vocabulary words listed. (See
    Vocabulary, below.)
*   Sing the song with the recording.

3. **Perform the movements with a rhythmic
    accompaniment/assess learning.** Have
    students:
    *   Perform the movements as they sing the song.
    *   Practice the following ostinato to accompany the
        song. (Use large woodblocks, slit drums, or log
        drums.)

    *   Divide into two groups: one group sings and moves
        as the other group plays the ostinato. Switch parts
        and repeat the song.

RESOURCES

Movement Variation
This song may also be performed
standing up. When repeating the song,
have students stand and use the same
arm motions. They should move their
knees with the beat, alternately
bending left and right knees.

Notation
Have students notate the following
measures (which you may wish to
sing for them) using the rhythmic
building blocks on **Visual Aid 38.**

Measures 1–2:

Measures 3–4:

♩ ♩♩ | ♩. ⅀ |
Ho - e a - na

Creative Movement
Have students choose a favorite rhyme
or song text and work in groups to
create movements that express the
meaning of the words. Groups could
each choose their own text, or agree in
advance to work on the same text and
compare solutions. Have groups
perform for each other.

Video Reference
See the *Share the Music* video "Music
and Movement" for a clip of Polynesian
dancers from the Cook Islands.

Vocabulary
hoe (**ho** e) = paddle
ana (ɑ nɑ) = let's
te (te) = the
vaka (**vɑ** kɑ) = canoe

Conversation Corner
Ia ora na. (ɪɑ o **rɑ** nɑ) = Hello.
Himene tatou. (hi **me** ne t'ɑ t'ou) =
  Let's sing together.
Na na. (**nɑ** nɑ) = Goodbye.

Hoe Ana Te Vaka
(Paddle the Canoe)

Tahitian Folk Song
Collected and Transcribed
by Kathy B. Sorensen

Copyright © 1991 Kathy B. Sorensen

SUK SAN WAN PI MAI
(New Year's Song)

Objective
Create movement to show phrases

Materials
Suk San Wan Pi Mai (New Year's Song):
    Laotian/English **CD1:35**; Pronunciation **CD1:36**
Visual Aid 21 (Song Map)
long strips of colored paper, crepe-paper
    streamers, or scarves

TEACHING THE LESSON

1. **Introduce the song.** Have students:
   • Discuss the best time in the year to celebrate the start of the New Year. Ask them what month they would choose if the New Year could start in any month, and have them tell why.
   • Make up appropriate greetings to wish friends a new year of good fortune.

2. **Teach the song.** Have students:
   • Listen to the song while following **Visual Aid 21.**
   • Listen again to locate the phrases in the song, telling how they know where a new phrase begins. (The phrases are separated by rests; if students follow the printed music, have them notice the eighth rests: ⁷)

   • On another listening, count the phrases and find two phrases that are alike. (four phrases; phrases 2 and 3)
   • Listen for and describe the pitches that are heard at the end of the recording. (The pitches repeat the last two notes of the song an octave higher.)
   • Listen to and practice the pronunciation of the words, following Visual Aid 21.
   • Practice saying the vocabulary words listed. (See **Vocabulary,** below.)
   • Echo-sing, then sing the song.

3. **Create movement/assess learning.** Have students:
   • Form a seated circle, holding strips of paper with printed New Year's greetings in each hand. (See **Language Arts** below, or use scarves or streamers.)
   • Choose a leader, who remains seated in the circle.
   • Sing the song, imitating the leader's movement of the paper streamers, changing the motion each time a new phrase begins.
   • Repeat the activity with a new leader and a new motion for each phrase.
   • Stand up, making a single line behind the leader. Follow around the classroom as the leader walks with the beat. Continue to imitate the leader's gestures with the streamers, changing on each phrase.

RESOURCES

Background
Nobody should expect to stay dry during *Pi Mai,* the Lao New Year. Not only are religious icons and temples washed, but friends and strangers are cheerfully ambushed and drenched with buckets of water during this celebration of cleansing and renewal.

Language Arts
Have students print New Year's greetings on long strips or streamers of colored paper. Use these with the movement activity. Have volunteers read some greetings aloud to share their New Year's sentiments, then decorate the classroom with the streamers.

Singing Harmony
Have students sing a harmony part on the last phrase with these pitches: B♭ B♭ C B♭ A♭ B♭ C B♭ A♭ G. Have students practice the harmony part first on bells, then vocally, playing and singing with accurate rhythm. Then divide the class into three groups, one to sing the melody, one to sing harmony, and the third to support the harmony on bells when the last phrase of the song is sung.

Web Site
For more about Laotian people and places, refer to this site:
http://www.laoembassy.com/discover/index.htm

Vocabulary
ໃໝ່ (maɪ) = new
ປີ (pi) = year
ວັນ (wɑn) = day

Conversation Corner
ສະບາຍດີ (sə baɪ di) = Hello./Goodbye.
ຂ້ອຍຊື່ _____ (kɔi sɯ _____) =
    My name is _____.
ເຊີຣ້ອງເພັງກັນ (sən hɔŋ pɛŋ gʌn) =
    Let's sing together.

The phonetics above do not reflect the nuances of this tonal language.

McGraw-Hill School Division

Suk San Wan Pi Mai

(New Year's Song)

Laotian Song
Collected and Transcribed by
Kathy B. Sorensen
English Version by MMH

Laotian: ວັນ ນີ້ ວັນ ດີ ປີ ໃໝ່ ເຮົາ ມາ ອວຍ ໄຫ້ ໃຫ້ ສຸກ ສ່າ ລາມ
Pronunciation: wan nɪ wan di pi maɪ haʊ ma 'ʋaɪ saɪ haɪ sʊk sam lan
English: To-day, to-day good New Year's Day, We wish you luck to-day!_

ຮ່ວຍ ສ້າງ ວັນ ນີ້ ໃຫ້ ເປັນ ແດນ ສະ ຫວັນ ຮ່ວຍ
rɔɪ sang wan ni haɪ pɛn dɛn sa wan rɔɪ
_ Come cel - e - brate_ with us,_____ Come

ສ້າງ ວັນ ນີ້ ໃຫ້ ເປັນ ແດນ ສະ ຫວັນ ມາ
sang wan ni haɪ pɛn dɛn sa wan ma
cel - e - brate_ with us,_____ Come

ຟ້ອມ ລຳ ກັນ ສະ ຫລອງ ວັນ ປີ ໃໝ່
fɔm lam kan sa lɔng wan pi maɪ
cel - e - brate a Hap - py New Year.

McGraw-Hill School Division

SAN LUN TSA
(Three-Wheeled Taxi)

Objective
Sing using dynamic variations

Materials
San lun tsa (Three-Wheeled Taxi):
  Mandarin/English **CD1:37**; Pronunciation
  CD1:38
Visual Aid 22 (Song Map)
unpitched wooden classroom instruments

TEACHING THE LESSON

1. **Introduce the song.** Have students:
    *   Make a list of the different modes of transportation they know about, including those from a variety of times and places.
    *   Listen to the song, following **Visual Aid 22.** Describe a three-wheeled taxi and how it works.

2. **Teach the song.** Have students:
    *   Listen to the song to hear the ♩♫ rhythmic patterns. Identify these patterns as three unequal sounds to a beat.
    *   Using the song notation, read the rhythm of the entire melody with rhythm syllables.
    *   Play the rhythm of the song on an unpitched wooden instrument, repeating the last three measures several times and getting softer with each repetition.
    *   Practice the pronunciation for the song.
    *   Practice saying the vocabulary words listed. (See **Vocabulary,** below.)
    *   Echo-sing, then sing the song.

3. **Sing using dynamic variations/assess learning.** Have students:
    *   Review dynamics and their symbols. (See **Dynamic Symbols,** below.)
    *   Practice singing the whole song at varying dynamic levels.
    *   Choose a different dynamic level for each measure, discussing appropriate dynamics for the English lyrics. (Write the chosen order on the board for reference. Optional: to simplify this activity, have students choose only two different dynamic levels, one for Measures 1–2 and another for Measures 3–4.)
    *   Sing the song using the chosen dynamic level for each measure. (Point to each dynamic symbol in turn on the board.)
    *   Suggest a different order for the dynamics, then sing the song using the new order.
    *   Sing the song, following the dynamics shown on Visual Aid 22.

RESOURCES

Dynamic Symbols
Have students review the names and meanings of the dynamic symbols *p*, *mp*, *mf*, *f* (*piano, mezzo piano, mezzo forte, forte*). Have volunteers list other dynamic symbols they know.

Movement
Have students form groups of three. One student stands in front and two others side by side, behind the leader. As they sing the song, they tiptoe eighth notes for the first three beats of each measure, stopping completely on the fourth beat. (*tiptoe, tiptoe, tiptoe, stop*)

Playing Instruments
Have students play the preceding movement pattern on D and A resonator bells as a chordal bordun accompaniment.

Chinese Characters
Have students notice that the first character in the song has three horizontal strokes. This character means "three." Tell them that a single horizontal stroke means "one" or "a" (Measure 3, fifth character). The character for "five" has five strokes, but they are not all horizontal (Measure 3, second character). This song's Chinese words humorously ask about someone who pays twice as much as necessary for a taxi ride.

Web Site
Use this site to see how to draw Chinese characters for numbers.
http://www.ocrat.com/ocrat/chargif/numbers.html

Vocabulary
三 (san) = three
輪 (luɛn) = wheel
車 (chər) = vehicle

Conversation Corner
您 好。(nin hao) = Hello.
您 好 嗎？(nin hao ma) = How are you?
謝 謝。(shiɛ shiɛ) = Thank you.

The phonetics above do not reflect the nuances of this tonal language.

McGraw-Hill School Division

San Lun Tsa
(Three-Wheeled Taxi)

Taiwanese Folk Song
Collected and Transcribed by Kathy B. Sorensen
English Version by MMH

Mandarin: 三 輪 車　　跑 得 快　　上 面 坐 個 老 太 太
Pronunciation: san luɛn chər　　pau di kwai　　san miɛn juɔ gər lau tai tai
English: **Shall I come?__ Shall I go?　East or West I do not know!**

要 五 毛　　給 一 塊　　你 說 奇 怪 不 奇 怪
yau wu mao　　gei yi kwai　　ni shuɔ chi gwai bu chi gwai
I am lost__ all a-lone,__ Three-wheeled tax-i,__ take me home!

KOROBUSHKA

Objective
Create body percussion to show ABB form

Materials
Korobushka: Russian/English **CD1:39**;
    Pronunciation **CD1:40**
Visual Aid 23 (Song Map)

TEACHING THE LESSON

1. **Introduce the song.** Have students:
   - Recall a familiar song that has only two sections to sing (AB form; any song in Verse-Refrain form), then try to remember a song that has two sections but goes back to the first (ABA).
   - Listen to the song and tell the main idea about the character in the song. (A peddler is showing his wares.)

2. **Teach the song.** Have students:
   - Listen again, patting the strong beat on the knees through the A section.
   - Identify the B section by patting the strong beat on the knees and the weak beat on the shoulders.

- Use **Visual Aid 23** to track the song, tapping gently with a finger on the tambourine pictures that represent strong and weak beats as they listen.
- Identify the section of the song that is repeated. (the B section)
- Tell which section begins with the higher pitches. (B)
- Tell how the form of the song could be expressed in letters. (ABB)
- Practice saying the Russian words, following the recorded pronunciation guide.
- Learn the vocabulary words listed. (See **Vocabulary,** below.)
- Sing the song.

3. **Create body percussion to show ABB form/assess learning.** Have students:
   - Create a two-beat pattern using body percussion to show a strong and weak beat.
   - Sing the song again, taking imaginary items out of an imaginary trunk to show the A section and performing their body percussion pattern to show the repeated B section.
   - Sing the song without the recording, accelerating the tempo as they progress through the B section to the end.

RESOURCES

Musical Instruments
Ask students to identify or describe the instruments heard on the recording. (small ensemble featuring violin, clarinet, tambourine) Point out that this type of ensemble is often associated with Eastern European folk music.

Playing Instruments
Have students create a tambourine accompaniment that reflects the ABB form.

Translation
Over the years, English singers of this song have used varied translations. Translated literally, the Russian words are those of a young man trying to win a girl over by offering her beautiful things from his trunk and

making her feel sorry for his tired shoulder.

Background
The Russian language is written in the Cyrillic alphabet. Two Orthodox missionaries, one named Cyril, developed the alphabet from Greek and Bulgarian systems in the 800s in order to better communicate with Slavic peoples.

Language Arts
Invite students to create additional verses that describe other items, from the categories of clothing, household goods, or tools, that a peddler might sell.

Community Connection
Have students visit a local Russian restaurant or community center. Students can practice the Russian greetings they have learned. They can also perform "Korobushka" for restaurant staff members or ask the staff to share Russian stories or songs.

Vocabulary
полна (pɔl **na**) = full
коробушка (kɔ **rɔ** bush kə) = trunk

Conversation Corner
Здравствуйте. (**zdrɑst** vui tyɛ) = Hello.
Меня зовут___. (min **yɑ** zɑ **vut**___) = My name is ___.
Спасибо. (spɑ **si** bə) = Thank you.
До свидания. (**dɑ** svi **dɑ** ni yɑ) = Goodbye.

Korobushka

Russian Folk Song
Russian Words by Nikolay Kekrasov
English Version by MMH

A

B7   **Em**

Russian: Ой,   пол - на,   пол - на   ко - ро - буш - ка,
Pronunciation: ɔi   pɔl   nɑ   pɔl   nɑ   kɔ   rɔ   bush   kə
English: "See   what   I   have   here   in   my   ko - ro - bush - ka!"

B7   **Em**   **Am**   **Em**

Есть   и   сит - цы   и   пар - ча.
yɛst   i   si   tsɪ   i   pɑɾ   cha
We   can   hear   the   ped - dler's   cry.

B

Am   **Em**

По - жа - лей   мо - я   за - зно - буш - ка
pɔ   зa   lye   mɑ   уa   za   zno   bush   kə
"I   am   on - ly   a   rag - ged   ped - dler, but
Lace   and   sat - in   and   col - ored   rib - bon, and

B7   **Em**   **Am**   **Em**

Мо - ло - дец - ко - го   пле - ча.
ma   la   dyɛts   ka   vɔ   plyɛ   cha
I   have   treas - ures   you   can   buy:
shin - y   beads   to   catch   your   eye!"

UA TXIAB

Objective
Sing individually and in groups

Materials
Ua Txiab: Hmong/English **CD1:41**; Pronunciation **CD1:42**
Visual Aid 24 (Song Map): prepare as a transparency (optional)
index cards numbered 1–4 (enough sets of four to have one card per student)
tape recorder (optional)

TEACHING THE LESSON

1. **Introduce the song.** Have students:
    *   Discuss ways that people show thanks and appreciation to each other. (Write a card or letter, give gifts, say "thank you.")
    *   Working in groups or as a class, enter words in the webs on **Visual Aid 24,** listing qualities and deeds of their fathers and/or mothers for which they are thankful. (Use a transparency for the class.)

2. **Teach the song.** Have students:
    *   Listen to the song, following Visual Aid 24 and raising hands on hearing a solo voice.
    *   Find on Visual Aid 24 the "nonsense" phrases that are sung by the whole group.
    *   Define "improvisation" and suggest ideas for improvised endings to the solo lines. (Improvising

is making up music while performing it. At first, have students improvise lyrics only, using the given solo melody and ideas from their word webs.)
    *   Practice improvising words to fit the solo measures. (Adjust the balance control to hear the recorded instrumental track only or use the instrumental verse provided.)
    *   Echo the recorded pronunciation guide to learn the Hmong words.
    *   Practice the vocabulary words listed. (See **Vocabulary,** below.)
    *   Listen to the song again, whispering along with the newly learned words.
    *   Sing the song with the recording.

3. **Sing individually and in groups/assess learning.** Have students:
    *   Define the terms *quartet* (four), *trio* (three), *duet* (two), and *solo* (one).
    *   Take a numbered index card, then form quartets with one card of each number.
    *   In these quartets, sing the solo lines of the song as written (not improvised). Then sing in trios by having 4s be seated, sing in duets after 3s are seated, and finally sing as soloists (1s only).
    *   Volunteer to improvise the solo lines as the group sings the other lines.
    *   Take turns recording and playing back their solo performances for the class.

RESOURCES

Vocal Development
Have the class discuss techniques to enhance solo singing: take a good preparatory breath, use correct posture, maintain proper focus, tune carefully, and enunciate clearly.

Hmong singers characteristically alternate between heavy and light voices as they sing their traditional songs, which often have large leaps and wide ranges. In improvising, Hmong singers use as many beats as desired to express their sentiments. If students wish to expand their improvisations, have them sing this song without accompaniment.

Background
This song is sung during the Hmong New Year. New Year festivities last from October until January: one clan or village celebrates it at a time so others may tour and take part. Dating teens sing this song to get acquainted; adults and children sing it to give thanks for the old year and to welcome the new.

Challenge Activity
The Hmong traditionally toss an orange back and forth with a partner as they sing this song. Invite students to gently toss an orange, tennis ball, or bean bag back and forth as they sing and take turns improvising.

Language Arts
Create additional verses thanking a brother, sister, or friend.

Vocabulary
xyoo nov (yōng nɔ) = this year
yuav mus muaj (yuɔ mu muɔ) = thankful for

Conversation Corner
Nyob zoo. (nyɔ ʒōng) = Hello.
Sawvdaws hu nkauj ua ke.
(shədə hu gu wɔ ge) = Let's sing together.
Mus zoo. (mu ʒōng) = Goodbye.

See CD2 for a recorded pronunciation of each phrase.

McGraw-Hill School Division

Ua Txiab

White Hmong Folk Song
Collected, Transcribed, and Arranged by Vilay Her
English Words by Linda Worsley

Hmong:	**Ua** _____ **txiab** _____	**niam**	**es,** _____
Pronunciation:	uwɔ tsiə	niə	ɛ
English:	**Ua** _____ **txiab** _____	**niam**	**es,** _____

Ca xyoo nov es yuav mus muaj ib tug mi txiv zoo __ le koj os
gya yŏng nɔ ɛ yuɔ mu muɔ i thu mi tsi ʒong le kʲɔ ɔ
1. This year I am thank-ful for a fa-ther like you, _good fa-ther,
2. This year I am thank-ful for a moth-er like you, _good moth-er,

ntuj	**es** _____	**os.**
thu	ɛ	ɔ
ntuj	*es* _____	*os.*
ntuj	*es* _____	*os.*

Ca xyoo nov es yuav mus muaj koj los khwv zaub mov __ rau peb noj
gya yŏng nɔ ɛ yuɔ mu muɔ kʲɔ lɔ ku ʒau cm dau bɛı nɔ
This year I am thank-ful you pro-vide us with food, _good fa-ther,
This year I am thank-ful that you care for us all, _good moth-er,

ntuj	**es** _____	**os.**
thu	ɛ	ɔ
ntuj	*es* _____	*os.*
ntuj	*es* _____	*os.*

*The ends of the "Solo" lines are improvised.
The "All" lines are nonsense words.

ARIRANG

Objective
Perform an instrumental countermelody

Materials
Arirang: Korean/English **CD1:43;** Pronunciation
   CD1:44
Visual Aid 25 (Song Map)
recorders or other melodic instruments

TEACHING THE LESSON

1. **Introduce the song.** Have students:
   - Recall texts from popular songs they know. (Suggest current hits or pop classics.)
   - Identify themes or topics that many of these songs have in common. (Many deal with friendship, love, and loss. Tell students that they will be learning a Korean folk song that shares these topics.)

2. **Teach the song.** Have students:
   - Listen to the song, following **Visual Aid 25.**
   - Discuss the meaning of the words. (Explain to students that the woman left behind by her loved one is not being mean-spirited when she hopes that he will suffer a foot ailment. She is expressing her deep wish that before he goes far, his foot will hurt and he will return to her.)

- Listen to the song in Korean and read the literal translation, found under the Korean on Visual Aid 25. (Explain that a *li* is about a quarter of a mile.)
- Compare the literal translation with the translation used in singing found at the bottom of the page. (The two are close in meaning.)
- Learn the Korean words by echoing the recorded pronunciation guide and following the song map.
- Learn the vocabulary words listed. (See **Vocabulary,** below.)
- Listen to the song again, whispering or softly singing learned vocabulary words.
- Sing the song with the recording.

3. **Teach a countermelody/assess learning.** Have students:
   - Look at the notation for the countermelody. (See **Countermelody,** below, and notate it on the board.)
   - Recall that a dotted half note is held for three beats.
   - "Chin" the countermelody on recorder. (Sing the letter names of the notes as they finger the notes on the recorder, with the mouthpiece resting on the chin. Note: this may also be played on keyboards, bells, or other pitched percussion instruments.)
   - Play the countermelody.
   - Divide into two groups, one group singing while the other plays the instrumental countermelody.
   - Repeat, with the groups switching parts.

RESOURCES

Countermelody

Playing Instruments
Have students learn this Orff accompaniment to "Arirang."

*tacet on Line 4

Vocabulary
고개 (go ge) = hill
발 (bal) = foot

Conversation Corner
안녕하세요? (an nyɔng ha sɛ yo)
  = How are you?
같이 노래합시다.
  (gat chi no ɾæ hap shi da) =
  Let's sing together.
고마와요. (go ma wa yo) = Thank
  you.
안녕. (an nyɔng) = Goodbye.

Arirang

Korean Folk Song
English Words by
Marilyn Davidson

Korean: 아 리 랑 아 리 랑 아 라 리 요
Pronunciation: a ɾi raŋ a ɾi raŋ a ɾa ɾi yo
English: A - ri- rang,— A - ri- rang,— A - ra - ri - yo.———

아 리 랑 고 개 를 넘 어 간 다
a ɾi raŋ go ge ɾul nɔ mɔ gan da
You are go-ing far a - way— o - ver A - ri-rang hill.

나 를 버 리 고 가 시 는 님 은
na ɾul pɔ ɾi go ga shi nɯn ni mɯn
Oh, my friend, if you leave me— here a - lone,— may your

십 리 도 못 가 서 발 병 난 다
shim ni do mo ka sɔ bal pyɔŋ nan da
feet be - gin to hurt be-fore you've e - ven walked the first mile!

TẾT TRUNG
(Children's Festival)

Objective
Play a countermelody and a harmonic accompaniment

Materials
Tết Trung (Children's Festival): Vietnamese/English **CD1:45**; Pronunciation **CD1:46**
Visual Aid 26 (Song Map)
Visual Aid 27 (Countermelodies)
Visual Aid 28 (Harmonic Accompaniment)
recorders or pitched percussion instruments; handbells, handchimes, or resonator bells

TEACHING THE LESSON

1. **Introduce the song.** Have students:
   - Think of an autumn celebration in which people light special lanterns. (Halloween)
   - Listen as you explain that this song is sung during a lantern festival in Vietnam. (See **Background,** below.)

2. **Teach the song.** Have students:
   - Listen to the song, following **Visual Aid 26.**
   - Learn the Vietnamese words by echoing the recorded pronunciation guide.
   - Practice the vocabulary words listed. (See **Vocabulary,** below.)

   - Listen to the song again, softly saying the words practiced.
   - Sing the song with the recording.

3. **Teach the accompaniments/assess learning.** Have students:
   - Read either of the countermelodies from **Visual Aid 27,** using recorders or pitched percussion instruments. (The two countermelodies differ in difficulty. The first one (A) has only two pitches and is a good introduction to low E for beginning recorder players. The two countermelodies may also be played together with the song.)
   - Perform one or both of the countermelodies with the recording.
   - Read the harmonic accompaniment from **Visual Aid 28** on handbells, handchimes, or resonator bells. (A Ring Touch (RT) is a rung staccato. Ring handbells close to the shoulder and damp immediately.)
   - Perform the harmonic accompaniment with the recording.
   - Decide how to use the accompaniments with the verses of the song.
   - Divide into three groups with one group singing, another playing one or both countermelodies, and the third playing the harmonic accompaniment.
   - Perform the song and accompaniments with the recording.
   - Switch parts and repeat.

RESOURCES

Background
Vietnamese myth tells of Chang E, the Moon Lady, and her moon palace. People in Vietnam honor the moon with a Mid-autumn Festival or Children's Festival. One tradition is a lantern procession in which children carry their brightly colored paper lanterns of many shapes.

Playing Drums
Have students play along with the drum sounds from the second English verse. On *tung,* strike the center for a strong sound; on *yin,* play near the edge for a lighter sound; and on *kak,* strike the wood body of the drum.

Invite students to use these sounds in creating their own rhythmic ostinatos to go with the song.

Art
Have students make lanterns by first decorating an 8 1/2" x 11" piece of construction paper or tagboard with crayons or markers. Next, fold it in half lengthwise and cut in from the folded edge as shown.

Open the paper, then make a cylinder and staple it at top and bottom. Add a paper strip handle.

Vocabulary
đèn (dɛn) = lantern
sao (sɑu) = star
cá (kɑ) = fish

Conversation Corner
Chào. (chɑu) = Hello.
Cùng hát chung nhau.
   (kùng hɑt chung nyɑu) = Let's sing together.
Xin chào. (sin chɑu) = Goodbye.

See CD2 for a recorded pronunciation of each phrase.

Tết Trung
(Children's Festival)

Vietnamese Song
Collected and Transcribed by
Kathy B. Sorensen
English Words by MMH

Vietnamese:	Tết trung thu rước đèn đi chơi.	Em rước đèn đi khắp phố phường.
Pronunciation:	tɛt trung tu ɾʊk dɛn di choi	ɛm ɾʊk dɛn di kap fo fʊng
English: **1.**	At Mid - au - tumn Fes - ti - val,	Walk a - round with lan - terns lit.
2.	Beau - ti - ful and full the moon,	At Mid - au - tumn Fes - ti - val.

Long vui sướng với	đèn trong tay	Em múa ca trong ánh trăng rằm.
lʌng vuι sʊng vơι	dɛn trʌng taι	ɛm muə ka trʌng ʌn trang ɾam
Take them all a - cross the town,	**Sing - ing to the au - tumn moon.**
Wait - ing for the moon to rise,	**I can hear the sound of drums,**

Đèn ông sao với	đèn cá chám.	Đèn thiên nga với đèn bướm bướm,
dɛn ʌng sau voι	dɛn ka cham	dɛn tιɛn nga voι dɛn bʊm bʊm
Lan - terns all in dif - fer - ent shapes,	**Lan - tern an - gel, lan - tern dream,**
Tung yin yin kak tung yin yin,	Tung yin yin kak tung yin yin.

em rước đèn này	đến cung trăng.	Đèn xanh lơ với đèn tím tím.
ɛm ɾʊk dɛn naι	dɛn kung trʌng	dɛn sʌn lə voι dɛn tim tim
Lan - tern fish, or lan - tern star,	**Lan - tern swan or but - ter - fly.**
I can hear the sound of drums,	Tung yin yin kak tung yin yin,

Đèn xanh lam với	đèn trắng trắng,	trong ánh đèn rực rỡ muôn màu.
dɛn sʌn lam voι	dɛn trʌng trʌng	trʌng ʌn dɛn ɾʊk ɾư mun mau
Take my lan - tern to the sky;	**Take my lan - tern to the moon.**
Tung yin yin kak tung yin yin.	Wel - come, la - dy in the moon!

McGraw-Hill School Division

PUNG NOY LOY KRATONG
(Full Moon Float)

Objective
Perform hand movements

Materials
Pung Noy Loy Kratong (Full Moon Float):
Thai/English **CD2:1**; Pronunciation **CD2:2**
Visual Aid 29 (Song Map)

TEACHING THE LESSON

1. **Introduce the song.** Have students:
   - Recall holidays where lighted candles or lanterns are part of the celebration. (Hanukkah, Christmas, Kwanzaa, Diwali, Tết Trung)
   - Listen as you read **Background,** below.
   - Think of experiences they would like to "float away" on such an occasion.

2. **Teach the song.** Have students:
   - Listen to the song, using **Visual Aid 29.**
   - Describe the mood and character of this song. (floating, gliding, peaceful)
   - Listen again and, with palms up, fingers curving toward floor and thumbs pointing up to sky, "float" hands left for eight beats. For the next eight beats, "float" hands right, with palms down and fingers and thumbs curved toward sky. Continue, changing direction and hand position every eight beats.
   - Listen again, practicing the movement.
   - Echo the recorded pronunciation guide.
   - Practice the vocabulary words listed. (See **Vocabulary,** below.)
   - Listen to the song, whispering the words.
   - Sing the song, moving cupped hands.

3. **Perform hand movements/assess learning.** Have students:
   - Stand with arms out to sides, slightly bent at elbows, and learn the following hand positions. Keep palms parallel to floor. (Explain that in classical Thai dance, both men and women use elegant hand motions.)
   Beat 1: Thumb and index finger touching, other fingers spread apart. Right palm up, left palm down.
   Beat 2: Switch position of palms so that right palm faces down, left palm faces up.
   Beat 3: Both palms up; fingers curve back toward floor and thumbs point up to sky.
   Beat 4: Both palms down; fingers and thumbs curve back toward sky.
   - Practice the movements in order slowly, then at the tempo of the song. (If desired, change motions on every other beat or on each measure.)
   - Sing the song and perform the movement.

RESOURCES

Background
The Thai festival of Loy Kratong occurs during a full moon in autumn. It is a time to forget, or "float away," one's faults of the past year. On Loy Kratong Day, people create floats, forming banana leaves to look like lotus blossoms. A candle, an incense stick, and sometimes flowers go inside. In the evening, people set their floats adrift in a river. They pray that the year's bad experiences depart and that the new year will bring happiness.

Challenge Movement
Have partners face each other. Both move with knees slightly bent, swaying body gracefully and bending head slightly from side to side. One partner (boy) walks clockwise around the other (girl), who turns so they remain facing. Boys extend arms to sides more while girls keep hand movements in front of chest. Finally, have all pairs form a large circle that moves clockwise as a whole while each pair continues to rotate, sway, and move hands.

Playing Instruments
Have students play finger cymbals with the beat. Alternate between muffled (+; damp sound by placing cups together) and openly ringing (o).

Art
Have students create "floats" by stapling together large leaves or leaf-shaped pieces of laminated construction paper. Secure small candles inside with a bit of clay.

Vocabulary
เดือน (dʉɑn) = moon
ดาว (dɑu) = stars

Conversation Corner
ผมชื่อ____ครับ (pom chʉ____krap ᵔ)
   = My name is ____. (male)
ดิฉันชื่อ____ค่ะ (di chan chʉ____ka)
   = My name is ____. (female)

The phonetics above do not reflect the nuances of this tonal language.

Pung Noy Loy Kratong
(Full Moon Float)

Thai Folk Song
Collected and Transcribed by
Kathy B. Sorensen
English Words by MMH

Copyright © 1991 Kathy B. Sorensen

HONG TSAI ME ME
(Rainbow Sister)

Objective
Choose and play an ostinato

Materials
Hong Tsai Me Me (Rainbow Sister):
   Mandarin/English **CD2:3**; Pronunciation **CD2:4**
Visual Aid 30 (Song Map)
resonator bells or Orff instruments

TEACHING THE LESSON

1. **Introduce the song.** Have students:
   - Describe rainbows they have seen in nature. Name a rainbow's colors. (red, orange, yellow, green, blue, indigo, violet)
   - Look at **Visual Aid 30** and listen while you explain that the first two Chinese characters together mean "rainbow" and individually mean "red" and "colorful."
   - Discuss what "rainbow" qualities a person might have. (Bright, cheerful, colorful personality; in the context of this song, "rainbow" means "beautiful.")

2. **Teach the song.** Have students:
   - Listen to the song, noticing the instrumental accompaniment.
   - Name the instrument played at the end of

Phrases 1, 2, and 4. (Finger cymbals; the other instruments are a bamboo flute and a zheng, one style of Chinese zither.)
   - Learn the Mandarin words by echoing the recorded pronunciation guide.
   - Study the vocabulary words listed. (See **Vocabulary,** below.)
   - Sing the song following Visual Aid 30.

3. **Play an ostinato/assess learning.** Have students:
   - Find two measures in the song that are melodically alike (Measures 1, 3) and two lines that are rhythmically alike (Lines 1, 2).
   - Choose one measure from the song to try as a melodic ostinato, first clapping the rhythm, then naming the absolute pitches, and finally singing the pattern on *la* or with solfege or hand signs.
   - Select several volunteers to play the chosen measure on pitched instruments, and supporting volunteers to sing the patterns with hand signs. Have the group sing the song, using the chosen measure twice through as an introduction.
   - Repeat with as many different measures as time allows, then select the one the class decides sounds best with the song.
   - Play a challenge game: one student (or the teacher) plays a measure from the song chosen at random; the class identifies it by reciting the words in rhythm.

RESOURCES

Movement
Have students create swaying, twirling movements with bright, solid-colored scarves to express the mood of the song. One possibility follows below:
Line 1: make a big arc slowly from right to left
Line 2: reverse the arc, moving slowly from left to right
Line 3: turn slowly to the left, making a circle overhead
Line 4: move scarves slowly from high overhead to the floor

Playing Instruments
Have students choose one measure per line during which to play the temple blocks or woodblocks. Invite them to plan a simple rhythm pattern to complement the chosen measures. Play a gong or cymbal on the first beat of each measure where the blocks are not played, and play finger cymbals on the quarter rests (end of Lines 1, 2, and 4).

Language Arts
Have the class create words to fit the ostinato measure they chose. Then have them sing the words as they perform the ostinato.

Video Reference
See the *Share the Music* video "Instrument Sounds" for a clip of a performance on the ch'in, another Chinese zither.

Vocabulary
紅 彩 (hɔng tsɑi) = rainbow
妹 妹 (me me) = sister

Conversation Corner
您 好。 (nin hɑo) = Hello.
您 好 嗎？ (nin hɑo mɑ) = How are you?
我 叫 _____。 (wɔ jiɑo _____)
   = My name is ____.
The phonetics above do not reflect the nuances of this tonal language.

Hong Tsai Me Me
(Rainbow Sister)

Chinese Folk Song
Collected and Transcribed by Kathy B. Sorensen
English Words by MMH

Mandarin: 紅 彩 妹 妹 嗯 噯 哎 喲
Pronunciation: hɔng tsai me me ʌn ai ei yo
English: 1. Rain - bow___ sis - ter,___ kind___ and good.
2. In the___ spring, with___ flow - ers bright.

長 得 那 麼 嗯 噯 哎 喲
jang də na mɔ ʌn ai ei yo
I would___ see her___ if___ I could.
I met___ sis - ter___ there___ one night.

櫻 桃 小 嘴 嗯 哎 呦 喲
ing tau shiau jwe ʌn ai ei yo
I can't for - get___ her,___ I don't know why,___
In the___ fall,___ when___ flow - ers die,___

一 點 點 那 麼 嗯 哎 呦 喲
i dien dien na mɔ ʌn ai ei yo
Think - ing of her,___ I al - ways cry.
Rain - bow sis - ter___ said___ good - bye.

Share World Music: Songs from Asia and Oceania for Grades K–6

NIM YOG XYOO NUAV
(In This Year)

Objective
Identify and perform grace notes

Materials
Nim Yog Xyoo Nuav (In This Year): Hmong/English
CD2:5; Pronunciation **CD2:6**
Visual Aid 31 (Song Map)

TEACHING THE LESSON

1. **Introduce the song.** Have students:
   - Discuss how folk songs are handed down from one generation to the next and thus connect the generations in the culture.
   - Name several folk songs they consider to be part of their cultural heritage.
   - Learn that because of numerous wars in their region, many Hmong people are orphans, creating a need for heightened personal and cultural connections.

2. **Teach the song.** Have students:
   - Listen to the song, following **Visual Aid 31.**
   - Discuss words of the text that offer insight into the Hmong culture and history. (Explain that the vocables *aws os* express sadness.)
   - Listen again, following the rhythm notation on Visual Aid 31 and noticing the ornamental pitches they hear before some notes. (♪; Identify these as grace notes.)
   - Listen as you demonstrate grace notes. (Play the first phrase of the song on a pitched instrument, emphasizing the embellishments.)
   - As the first phrase is played again, raise a hand upon hearing each grace note.
   - Echo the Hmong words, using the recorded pronunciation guide.
   - Practice the vocabulary words listed. (See **Vocabulary,** below.)
   - Echo-sing the song phrase by phrase, then sing the song with the recording.

3. **Identify and perform grace notes/assess learning.** Have students:
   - Refer to the printed music to find the first grace note. (small note with a line through it; second note in Measure 2)
   - Locate two grace notes side by side in one measure. (Measure 11)
   - Practice singing grace notes both above and below the regular note after hearing the necessary pitches. (Measures 2, 3)
   - Sing the song, performing the grace notes.
   - Sing the song, pointing to the grace notes in the printed music.
   - Repeat the song, tapping the rhythms of the grace notes as they occur.
   - Volunteer to perform the last phrase as a solo, adding a grace note as desired.

RESOURCES

Game
Materials: Visual Aid 31, one number cube or set of number cards, one game piece per player, score-keeping materials

Instructions: Two or more players take turns rolling a number cube (or turning up number cards from a central pile) and moving game pieces around the track as the numbers dictate. Students accrue points according to the note values on which they land: eighth note = half, quarter note = one, dotted quarter = one and one-half, half note = two, and so on. A rest earns no points but a grace note adds an extra 10 points to the player's score.

Composition
Have students create a 16-beat melody (four measures in $\frac{4}{4}$) with lyrics and two grace notes.

Background
This Hmong folk song is a reminder to share prosperity. It asks for grace from heaven and earth in order to prosper. The reference in the lyrics to *rice, sweet rice, and wheat* convey how lucky some are to have three kinds of grain to eat.

Vocabulary
nruag (duɔ) = orphan
nam (nɑ) = mother
txiv (tsi) = father

Conversation Corner
Nyob zoo. (nyɔ ʒōng) = Hello.
Kuv lub npe hu ua___.
   (kˉu lu beι hu wɔ___) = My name is ____.
Sib ntsib dua lawm zag.
   (shi ji duɔ lə ʒɑ) = See you next time.

See CD2 for a recorded pronunciation of each phrase.

Nim Yog Xyoo Nuav
(In This Year)

Green Hmong Folk Song
Collected and Transcribed by Vilay Her
English Words by Linda Worsley

Hmong: Es nim yog xyoo nuav _____ miv ntxhais
Pronunciation: ɛ ni yɔ yõng nuɔ mi tsɑu
English: **Es nim yog** This year _____ lit-tle girl,

hluas nkauj. Nam tub nroj tub nruag aws os.
hluɔ gɑu na thu dɔ thu duɔ ə ɔ
young girl, **Or-phan, child of grass, aws os.**

Cag es lub ntuj lub teb yuav moog
gya ɛ lu lu thu lu theu yuɔ mõng
Why is heav'n so dark, the earth, the

tsaus ntuj tsaus nti aws _____ os.
tsɑu ðu tsɑu thi ə ɔ
sky, the ground so dark, aws os?

Cag es hluag muaj nam hab muaj txiv nyob es
gya ɛ hluɔ muɔ na ha muɔ tsi nyɔ ɛ
Why have some a moth-er, some a fa-ther?

hluag tau mov nplej mov nplaum tshaab noj aws _____ os.
hluɔ thɑu mɔ bleu mɔ blɑu tsa nɔ ə ɔ
Some have rice, sweet rice, and wheat to eat, aws os!

FUNG YANG SONG

Objective
Sing a song in two parts and play a rhythmic accompaniment

Materials
Fung Yang Song: Chinese/English **CD2:7**;
   Pronunciation **CD2:8**
Visual Aid 32 (Song Map)
small hand drums and other unpitched
   instruments

TEACHING THE LESSON

1. **Introduce the song.** Have students:
   - Describe parades and street performances they have seen and tell how each type of event helps celebrate a special occasion.

2. **Teach the song.** Have students:
   - Listen to the song, raising the left hand when they hear a drum in the accompaniment.
   - Listen again, raising the right hand when they hear a cymbal.
   - Review and differentiate between a *countermelody* and a *round* or *canon*. (Both produce harmony. A countermelody is a second melody sung with the main melody; it contrasts with the main melody. A round or canon is the same melody sung starting at different times.)
   - Listen to the song again and describe differences between its melody (top line) and countermelody. (For example, this countermelody uses notes of longer duration and only uses two pitches.)
   - Follow **Visual Aid 32** as they echo the recorded pronunciation guide, then practice the vocabulary words listed on the right side of the visual aid.
   - Give reasons why the Chinese and English words are the same in the last two lines of text. (The words are vocables, or "nonsense syllables," that have no literal meaning but imitate instrument sounds.)
   - Sing the song (melody only) with the recording, then practice the countermelody.
   - Sing the song in two parts.

3. **Play a drum accompaniment/assess learning.** Have students:
   - Listen to the drum part for the A section, following it on Visual Aid 32 as they hear the recording once more.
   - Tap the drum part lightly in their palms as they listen again. (Repeat as needed, transferring to drums when students become secure.)
   - Volunteer to play the notated patterns on the drum as the class sings the song.

RESOURCES

Create a Celebration
Have the class plan a "street" (or school hallway) parade to celebrate a special event. Include simple costumes, banners, instruments, and singing.

B Section Accompaniment
Challenge students to add this drum part.

Language Arts
Invite students to create new words for the countermelody.

Playing Instruments
Have students practice and play the last two lines of the song on these suggested instruments:
drr = drum roll
ling = finger cymbal or small gong
tang = triangle
piao = drum (strike once)
yi = woodblock

Create an Accompaniment
Have students:
1. Divide into four groups; each selects a leader and a notetaker.
2. Put a large sheet of paper on the wall or board for each group. Divide each sheet into 15 boxes or measures. Decide whether to write instrumental parts in standard notation or to devise their own.
3. Create, notate, and practice a percussion accompaniment.
4. Perform the accompaniments by group as the other groups sing the song in two parts.

Vocabulary
See right side of Visual Aid 32.

Conversation Corner
您好。(nin hao) = Hello.
大家一起唱。(da jar i chi tsɔng)
   = Let's sing together.
再見。(tsai jiən) = Goodbye.

The phonetics above do not reflect the nuances of this tonal language.

Fung Yang Song

Chinese Folk Song
Arranged by
Marilyn Davidson

ÜSKÜDAR

Objective
Create a rhythmic accompaniment

Materials
Üsküdar: Turkish/English **CD2:9**; Pronunciation **CD2:10**
Visual Aid 33 (Song Map)
Visual Aid 34 (Rhythmic Building Blocks)
hand drums or other non-pitched percussion

TEACHING THE LESSON

1. **Introduce the song.** Have students:
   - Name the language from which the words *yogurt, kabob,* and *pasha* come. (Turkish)
   - Practice patting the following ostinato from notation on the board.

   - Pat the ostinato as they listen to the song.

2. **Teach the song.** Have students:
   - Rearrange the rhythms of the ostinato above, creating a new pattern of their own.

- Pat the new ostinato as they listen to the song again. Practice this again as needed.
- Using **Visual Aid 33,** discuss the rhythm combinations that make up each beat of the song. (dotted eighth-sixteenth, eighth note pair, four sixteenths, eighth and two sixteenths, two sixteenths and eighth, half note)
- Listen to and practice the pronunciation of the words while following Visual Aid 33.
- Learn the vocabulary word listed. (See **Vocabulary,** below.)
- Echo-sing the phrases of the song, led by you or a strong singer, then sing the song with the recording.

3. **Combine singing with accompaniment/ assess learning.** Have students:
   - Work in groups to create a non-pitched percussion part with two repeating eight-beat phrases. Cut out and arrange the rhythmic building blocks on **Visual Aid 34** to fill the two rows of blank boxes. Make the last beat of the second phrase a quarter note.
   - Transfer the new rhythmic accompaniment to body percussion, then to non-pitched percussion instruments, and perform it with the recording.
   - Sing the song with the rhythmic accompaniment.

RESOURCES

Notation
Have students use Visual Aid 34 to create a second layer of non-pitched percussion to accompany the song.

Playing Instruments
1. Have students learn to play the melodic accompaniment below on bells, keyboard, or recorder. Recorder players should first "chin" the accompaniment by resting recorder mouthpieces on their chins as they sing the pitch names and finger the notes.

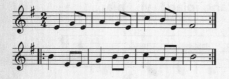

2. Play the accompaniments with the song. Divide into three groups, one to sing and one to perform each accompaniment learned. Sing the song several times, adding one more accompaniment each time.

Translation
A literal translation of the Turkish words is "While going to Üsküdar, it suddenly started to rain. My clerk's coat is long and its skirt got muddy." Üsküdar is a suburb of Istanbul.

Background
The modern Turkish alphabet was established by the government of 1928. It replaced the centuries-old written language of Ottoman Turkey, which had used Arabic characters and Arabic and Persian grammar.

Vocabulary
yağmur (ya mur) = rain

Conversation Corner
Merhaba. (**mer** ha ba) = Hello.
Benim adım___. (be **num** a d**ʌm**___) = My name is ____.
İyi günler. (i yi gün lɛr) = Goodbye.

Üsküdar

Popular Turkish Song
English Version by MMH

Turkish: Üs - kü - dar' a gi - der— i ken al - di - da bir yağ mur,
Pronunciation: üs kü daɾ a gi dɛɾ i kɛn ɑl di dɑ bir yɑ muɾ
English: Üs - kü - dar, a dis - tant— cit - y. I walk a-long the road.

Ka - ti - bi - min se - tre - si u - zun e - te - gi - ça-
ka ti bi min sɛ tɾɛ si u zun ɛ tɛ gi ja
On a rain-y morn - ing— there— I met— my—

mur. e - te - gi - ça - mur.
muɾ ɛ tɛ gi ja muɾ
friend. there— I— met— my— friend.

DIWALI SONG

Objective
Create a rhythm pattern in $\frac{6}{8}$

Materials
Diwali Song: Hindi/English **CD2:11**; Pronunciation **CD2:12**

Recorded Lesson: Playing Indian Music on the Tabla **CD2:13**

Visual Aid 35 (Song Map)

Visual Aid 36 (Rhythmic Building Blocks)

TEACHING THE LESSON

1. **Introduce the song.** Have students:
   - Discuss ways that they celebrate the New Year in their own homes or communities.
   - Learn about Diwali (see **Background,** below).

2. **Teach the song.** Have students:
   - Follow **Visual Aid 35** as they listen to the song. (The top part of the page shows the literal meaning of the words in the Hindi song text. The English text heard on the recording is printed at the bottom.)
   - Sing the melody with the recording, using the syllable *la.*
   - Echo the Hindi words using the recorded pronunciation guide. (Students may want to follow the Visual Aid as they practice the words.)
   - Practice the vocabulary words listed. (See **Vocabulary,** below.)
   - Sing the song with the recording.

3. **Create a rhythmic accompaniment/assess learning.** Have students:
   - Listen to the recorded lesson, "Playing Indian Music on the Tabla," to hear some examples of percussion rhythms.
   - Work in pairs, using **Visual Aid 36** to create an eight-beat rhythmic ostinato to accompany "Diwali Song." Cut out rhythmic building blocks and arrange them in the row of open boxes.
   - Divide into two groups with one group singing and the other group playing a rhythmic ostinato on hand drums. (Choose one ostinato from those created.)
   - Notice how many times the ostinato must be played to accompany the song. (7)
   - Trade jobs until each group's rhythmic ostinato has been performed.
   - Evaluate results. (Which patterns fit best with the melody? Which ones contrasted enough so that they could be heard? Did any of the patterns seem to overpower the melody? If so, how could they be improved?)

RESOURCES

Background
Diwali is the name of a Hindu festival that comes in late October or early November. Diwali usually coincides with the end of the Indian rainy season. The festival lasts from three to ten days, depending on local customs.

Diwali is a very joyful holiday because it marks the beginning of a new year. Lights are kept lit throughout Diwali, so that Lakshmi, the Hindu goddess of prosperity, can find her way to every home.

The name of the festival is derived from the Sanskrit word *Dipawali,* literally, "row of lights." Hundreds of *dipa* lamps, small clay saucers with cotton wicks, are lit. Today electric lights and candles are used as well as *dipa* lamps, and Indian villages glow with thousands of flickering lights throughout the days of Diwali. Public firework displays form an important part of the celebration in many communities.

On the morning of the principal day of Diwali, families enjoy a festive breakfast together. Afterwards they visit friends and exchange gifts of special sweets.

Video Reference
See the *Share the Music* video "Blending Musical Styles" for a clip of Ravi Shankar, sitar, and Yehudi Menuhin, violin, performing together.

Vocabulary
खुशी (**ku** shi) = happy

दीप (**di** pə) = clay oil lamp

Conversation Corner
नमस्ते (na mas te) = Hello./Goodbye.

मेरा नाम____ (mɛ **ra nam**___) = My name is _____.

हम सब एक साथ गायें (hʌm sab ek sat gaɪn) = Let's sing together.

धन्यवाद (**dan** yə **vad**) = Thank you.

Diwali Song

Collected by
Kathy B. Sorensen
As sung by Chhanda Chakroborti

McGraw-Hill School Division

NIAM ES

Objective
Create a rhythmic accompaniment for the B and C sections of a rondo

Materials
Niam Es: Hmong/English **CD2:14**; Pronunciation **CD2:15**
Visual Aid 37 (Song Map)
Orff instruments (soprano, alto, and bass xylophones; gongs; temple blocks)
unpitched instruments
map of Asia or the world

TEACHING THE LESSON

1. **Introduce the song.** Have students:
   - Look at a map to locate southeast Asia and name the countries found on that peninsula. (Vietnam, Laos, Cambodia, Thailand, part of Myanmar)
   - Listen as you introduce the Hmong people. (The Hmong are one of many groups in southeast Asia with their own language and culture. They live in China, Vietnam, Laos, and Myanmar. The Hmong helped the United States during the Vietnam War, and afterwards thousands of Hmong from Laos became refugees and moved to the U.S.)
   - Discuss what it might be like to live through a war or to become a refugee. (scary and disturbing—fighting, disruption of life; sad and lonely—people die, neighbors and friends go to other places)

2. **Teach the song.** Have students:
   - Listen to the song as they follow **Visual Aid 37**.
   - Listen as you explain that the Hmong, like many other people, express their emotions through songs.

In this song, a lonely young Hmong man is thinking of the loved one he has left behind. The vocables *niam es* express sadness or longing.
   - Listen to the song again to hear the vocal slides. (These are where the voice slides downwards, sometimes to an indeterminate pitch; unlike a glissando, not every pitch is sounded.)
   - Discuss how the slides add to the expressiveness of the song. (add sad sighing or moaning sound)
   - Find the printed symbol that indicates a slide. (downward diagonal line)
   - Notice that the song is in Rondo form. The A section begins and ends the song and occurs between each contrasting section.
   - Count the number of measures in the B and C sections. (B–6; C–8. This song is traditionally extended with many sections; each succeeding section is longer and adds new ideas.)
   - Learn the Hmong pronunciation by using the recorded guide.
   - Practice the vocabulary words listed. (See **Vocabulary,** below.)
   - Sing the song, following Visual Aid 37.

3. **Play an instrumental accompaniment/ assess learning.** Have students:
   - Learn the A section accompaniment. (See **Playing Instruments,** below.)
   - Divide into two groups to create their own unpitched instrumental parts to accompany the B and C sections. (Note that the Hmong emphasize Beats 2 and 4 in their traditional accompaniments.)
   - Perform the entire song with everyone singing the A section and the B and C groups singing and playing their sections. (Xylophone parts may be continued throughout the song.)

RESOURCES

Background
This song is from the White Hmong tribe. Each Hmong tribe, or group, is named according to the color of dress worn by its women. Other Hmong groups include Green, Striped, Flowery, Black, Red, and Blue. Each group speaks a different Hmong dialect, but most Hmong can understand the various dialects.

Playing Instruments

Vocabulary
paj (ba) = flower
xyoo nov (yŏng nɔ) = this year

Conversation Corner
Nyob zoo. (nyɔ ʒŏng) = Hello.
Kuv lub npe hu ua___.
   (kˈu lu beɩ hu wɔ___) =
   My name is ____.
Mus zoo. (mu ʒŏng) = Goodbye.

See CD2 for a recorded pronunciation of each phrase.

Niam Es

White Hmong Folk Song
Collected and Transcribed by Vilay Her
English Words by Linda Worsley

McGraw-Hill School Division

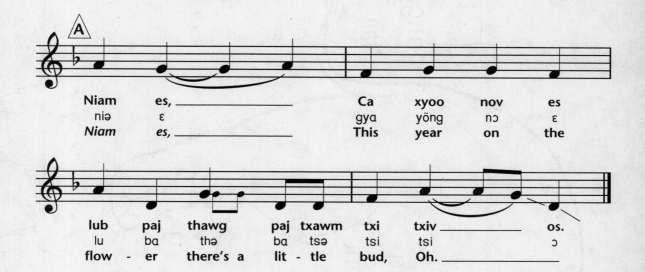

Niam   es, _____   Ca   xyoo   nov   es
niə   ε   gyɑ   yõng   nɔ   ε
Niam   es, _____   **This   year   on   the**

lub   paj   thawg   paj   txawm   txi   txiv _____ os.
lu   bɑ   thə   bɑ   tsə   tsi   tsi   ɔ
flow - er   there's a   lit - tle   bud,   Oh. _____

VISUAL AID 1 • Song Map

Chang
(Elephant)

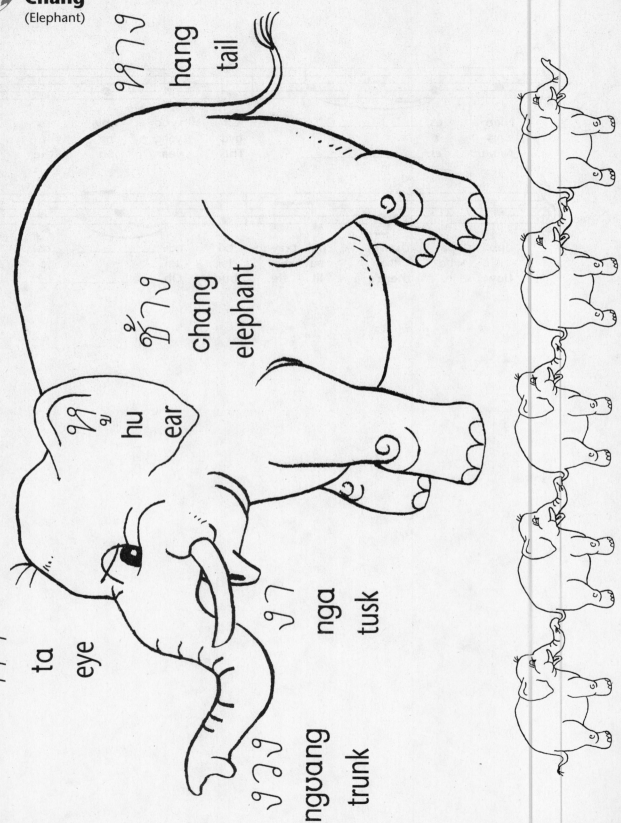

หาง
hang
tail

ช้าง
chang
elephant

หู
hu
ear

งา
nga
tusk

ตา
ta
eye

งวง
nguang
trunk

Share World Music: Songs from Asia and Oceania for Grades K–6

Name _____

Maliit Na Gagamba
(Little Spider)

gagamba
spider

ulan
rain

araw
sun

masaya
happy

Share World Music: Songs from Asia and Oceania for Grades K–6

Shiau Ya
(Little Duck)

游
yu
swim

小　鴨
shiau ya
little duck

母　鴨
mu ya
mother duck

Name _____

Shiau Ya
(Little Duck)

swim	swim	swim	swim
swim	gwa	gwa	
swim	swim	swim	swim
swim	gwa	gwa	
swim	gwa	swim	gwa
swim	gwa	gwa	
swim	gwa	swim	gwa
swim	gwa	gwa	

Kaeru No Uta
(Frog's Song)

Japanese: か え る の う た が
Pronunciation: ka e ɾu no u ta ga
English: Hear the frog, he sings a song.

き こ え て く る よ
ki ko e te ku ɾu yo
It is such a hap-py song:

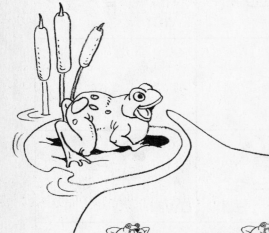

グワ   グワ   グワ   グワ
gwa   gwa   gwa   gwa
gwa   gwa   gwa   gwa

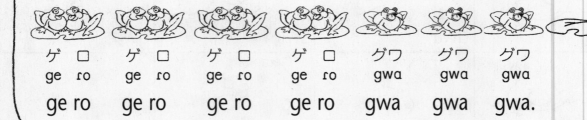

ゲ ロ   ゲ ロ   ゲ ロ   ゲ ロ   グワ   グワ   グワ
ge ɾo   ge ɾo   ge ɾo   ge ɾo   gwa   gwa   gwa
ge ro   ge ro   ge ro   ge ro   gwa   gwa   gwa.

Name _____

Sarika Kaio
(Myna Birds)

Cambodian:	សារិ កា កែវ អ្ញើយ
Pronunciation:	saɾi k̟a k̟a əi
English:	Oh, myna birds,

ស៊ី អ៊ី កង កង (ហេ សា រិ យុង)
si əi k̟ɔng k̟ɔng (haɪ sa ɾi yong)
eating plums in the tree, (la, la, la, la)

ស៊ី ផ្លែ ដាំ បង ប្រ ចិក គ្នា លេង អ្ញើយ អ្ញើយ
si plaɪ dam bɔng pɾɔ jʌkŋ kniə leng əi əi
And pecking one another playfully.

កែវ អ្ញើយ ស្លាប់ វា ចាក់ ក្បាច់ មាត់ វា ធ្វើ
k̟aɪo əi sla viə jak batʼŋ mɔtʼŋ viə twə
And your wings are dancing, moving to the sound,

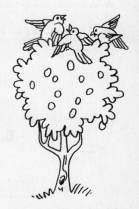

ភ្លេង (ហេ សា រិ យុង) ប្រ ចឹក គ្នា លេង ក្នុង ព្រៃ ប្រឹក សា
pleng (haɪ sa ɾi yong) pɾɔ jʌk kniə leng kn̟ong pɾɛɪ bɾun sa
As your beaks, (la, la, la, la) are making music all around,

អ្ញើយ អ្ញើយ កែវ អ្ញើយ
əi əi k̟aɪo əi
from high in the tree.

VISUAL AID 7 • Song Map

Sasara Ang Bulaklak
(The Flower Fades)

A

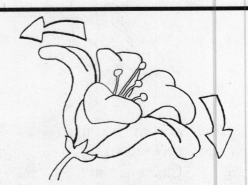

Tagalog: **Sasara ang bulaklak,**
English: Close the flower,

Bubuka ang bulaklak,
Open the flower,

Iikot ang bulaklak,
Turn the flower,

Dadaan ang reyna.
Make way for the Queen.

B

Bum ti ya ya, bum ti ya ya, bum ti ya ya ye ye

Bum ti ya ya, bum ti ya ya, bum ti ya ya ye ye a **bom!**

English Song Text

In the fall the flower fades, In the spring the flower blooms,
Now the flower turns around, Make way for the Queen now.

Name _____

Lek Kansaing
(Hiding the Towel)

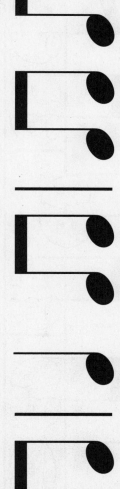

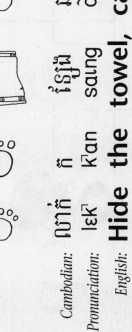

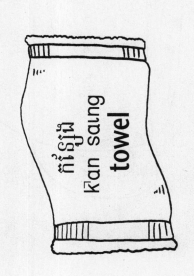

Cambodian:	ญาก้	ก้	แกงกั	ก
Pronunciation:	lɛk	kʻan	saing	
English:	**Hide**	**the**	**towel,**	**catch the cat, me - ow, me - ow.**

VISUAL AID 9 • Song Map

Nabe, Nabe, Soko, Nuke
(Stewpot, Stewpot, Bottomless Pot)

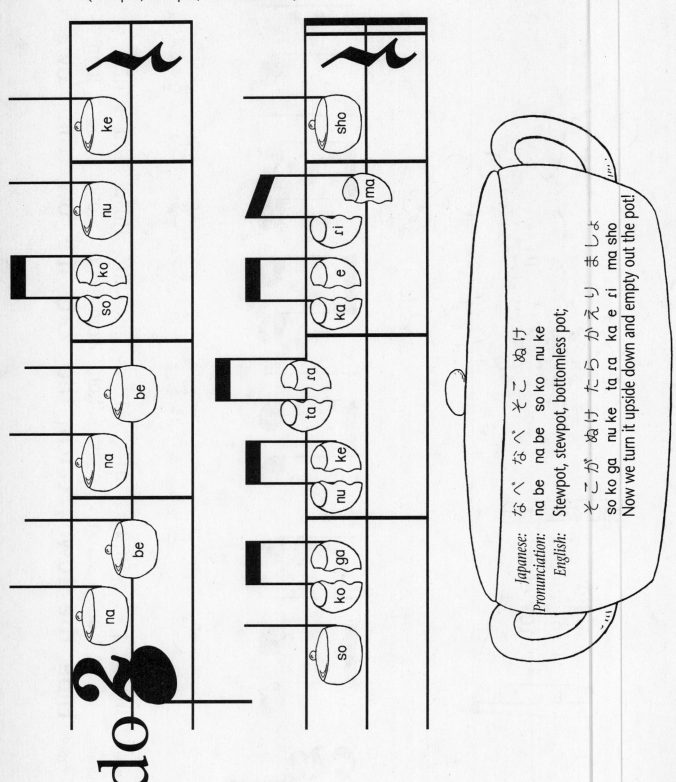

Japanese: なべ なべ そこ ぬけ
Pronunciation: na be na be so ko nu ke
English: Stewpot, stewpot, bottomless pot;

そこが ぬけ たら かえり ました
so ko ga nu ke ta ra ka e ri ma sho
Now we turn it upside down and empty out the pot!

Tang Tang Juen
(Round, Round, Turn)

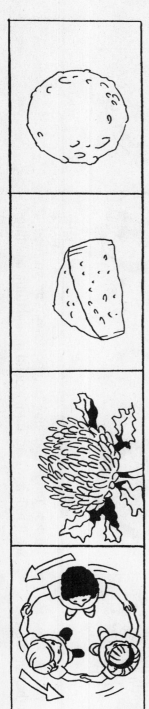

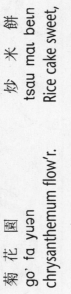

Cantonese: 糯呀糯米團
Pronunciation: lo a lo mɑɪ tuen
English: sticky rice to eat.

炒 米 餅
tsɑu mɑɪ ben
Rice cake sweet,

菊 花 園
go' fɑ yuen
chrysanthemum flow'r.

丞 丞 轉
tang tang juen
Round, round turn;

五月 初 五 係 籠 舟 節 呀
m yu chɔ m hɑɪ lɔn tsɑu tsi ɑ
May the fifth is the day of the dragon boats.

阿 媽 佢 叫 我 去 瞄 籠 船
a ma kɔɪ giu o–ɔ hɔɪ tɑɪ lɔn shen
Mother says, "Go and see, Go see the dragon boats."

雞 仔 大 我 吶 去 賣
gɑɪ tsɑɪ dɑɪ o le hɔɪ mɑɪ
When they're grown I'll take them, take them to sell.

我 唔 去 瞄 我 要 去 瞄 雞 仔
o m hɔɪ tɑɪ o yu hɔɪ tɑɪ gɑɪ tsɑɪ
"No, I would rather watch my little baby chickens!"

Tang Tang Juen
(Round, Round, Turn)

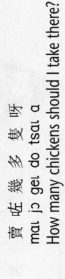

賣咗幾多隻呀
mɑɪ jɔ geɪ do tsɐɪ ɑ
How many chickens should I take there?

賣得幾多錢
mɑɪ dʌ geɪ do tsin
How much money will I make there?

佢轉得好好瞭
kɔɪ chun dʌ ho ho tɑɪ
When it turns, it's beautiful to see!

我有隻風車仔
o yɑu tsɐɪ fong cheɪ tsɐɪ
I have a little windmill.

瞭佢乙乙 tang tang juen
tɑɪ kɔɪ tang tang juen
See it round, round, turn;

瞭佢乙乙轉呀乙乙轉又轉
tɑɪ kɔɪ tang tang juen tɑng ɑ juen juen ɑ juen
See it round, round, turn, around, round, turn, and turn.

瞭佢乙 tang tang juen
tɑɪ kɔɪ tang tang juen
See it round, round, turn,

菊花園
go' fɑ yuen
chrysanthemum flow'r.

McGraw-Hill School Division

Chuột Cấp Trứng
(The Mouse and the Egg)

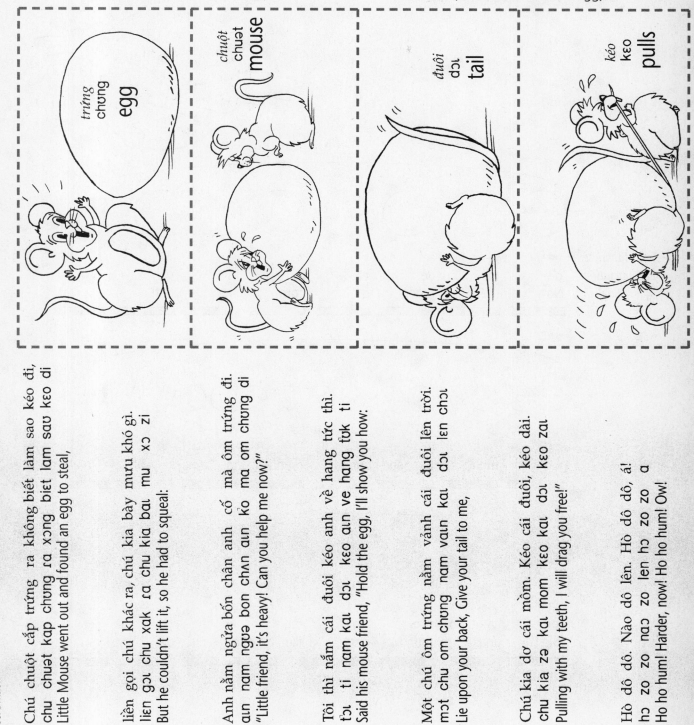

trứng
chung
egg

chuột
chuọt
mouse

đuôi
đɔı
tail

kéo
kɛo
pulls

Vietnamese: Chú chuột cấp trứng ra không biết làm sao kéo đi,
Pronunciation: chu chuọt kạp chưng ɾa xɔng biet lam sɑu kɛo di
English: Little Mouse went out and found an egg to steal,

liền gọi chú khác ra, chú kia bày mưu khó gì.
liən gɔı chu xɑk ɾa chu kiɑ bɑı mɯ cx zi
But he couldn't lift it, so he had to squeal:

Anh nằm ngửa bốn chân anh cố mà ôm trứng đi.
an nam ngɯɑ bon chɑn an kɔ ma om chưng di
"Little friend, it's heavy! Can you help me now?"

Tôi thì nằm cái đuôi kéo anh về hang tức thì.
tɔı ti nam kɑı đɔı kɛo an ve hang tɯk ti
Said his mouse friend, "Hold the egg, I'll show you how:

Một chú ôm trứng nằm vảnh cái đuôi lên trời.
mɔt chu om chưng nam vɑın kɑı đɔı len chɔı
Lie upon your back, Give your tail to me,

Chú kia dơ cái mồm. Kéo cái đuôi, kéo dài.
chu kiɑ zə kɑı mom kɛo kɑı đɔı kɛo zɑı
Pulling with my teeth, I will drag you free!"

Hò dô dô. Nào dô lên. Hò dô dô, â!
hɔ zo zo nɑo zo len hɔ zo zo ɑ
Ho ho hum! Harder, now! Ho ho hum! Ow!

McGraw-Hill School Division

Deta, Deta
(The Moon)

あ　る　い　ma　ru　i
つ　き
tsu ki
moon
round

Japanese:	で	た	で	た	つ	き	が
Pronunciation:	de	ta	de	ta	tsu	ki	ga
English:	Now	the	moon	is	com -	ing	out!

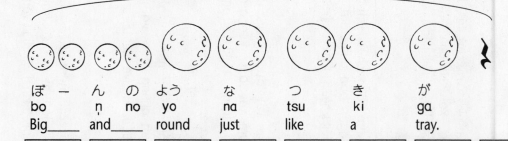

ま	ー	る	い	ま	ー	る	い	ま	ん	ま	る	い
ma		ɾu	i	ma		ɾu	i	ma	n̩	ma	ɾu	i
Big and		round, so		big	and	round, as		round___	as		a	tray.

ぼ	ん	の	よう	な	つ	き	が
bo	n̩	no	yo	na	tsu	ki	ga
Big____	and____	round	just	like	a		tray.

2. Now the moon is hiding!
   Gone away, O gone away, Behind the clouds.
   Black as ink, behind the clouds.

Wang Ü Ger

(Chinese Fishing Song)

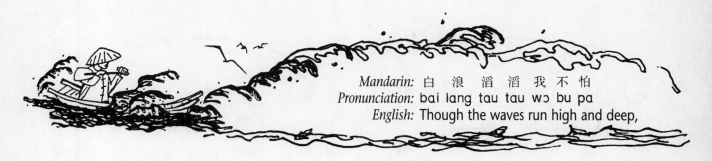

Mandarin: 白 浪 滔 滔 我 不 怕
Pronunciation: bai lang tau tau wɔ bu pa
English: Though the waves run high and deep,

掌 穩 舵 兒 往 前 划
jang wɛn duɔ ər wang chiɛn hwa
We sail on the course we keep.

撒 網 下 水 到 魚 家
sa wang sia shue dau yü jia
Throw the net and let it fall,

捕 條 大 魚 笑 哈 哈
bu tiau da yü siau ha ha
Catch the biggest fish of all.

Wang Ü Ger

(Chinese Fishing Song)

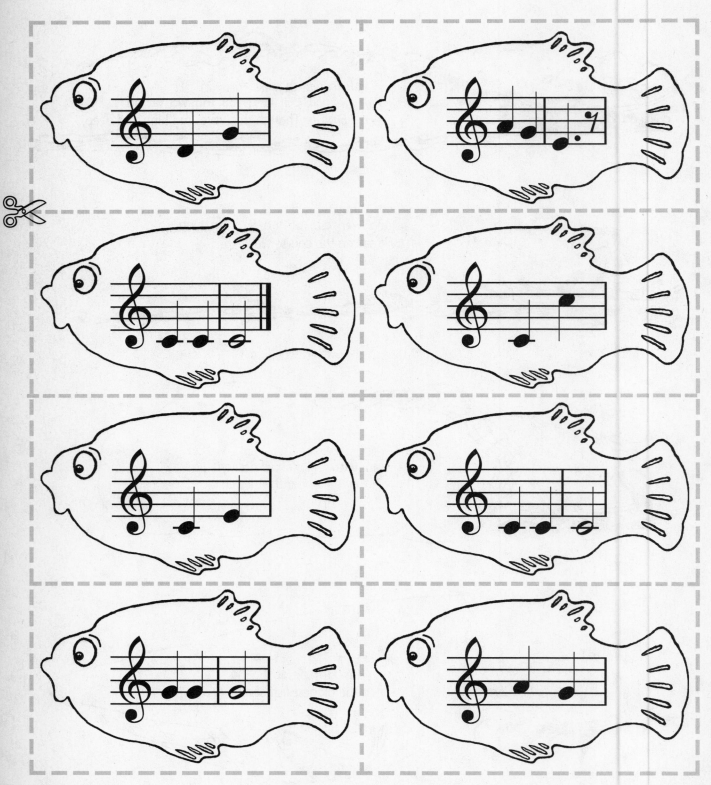

Name _____

Tititorea
(Maori Stick Game)

| Maori: | E | hi- | ne | ho- | ki | mai | ra. |
| Pronunciation: | e | hi | ne | ho | ki | maɪ | ɾɑ |

| E | pa- | pa | wai- | a- | ri | ta- | | ku nei | ma- | | hi, |
| e | pɑ | pɑ | waɪ | ɑ | ɾi | tɑ | | ku neɪ | mɑ | | hi |

| ta- | | ku nei | ma- | | hi | tu- | ku roi | | ma | ta. | Au |
| tɑ | | ku neɪ | mɑ | | hi | tu | ku ɾɔɪ | | mɑ | tɑ | ɑu |

| e | | au | e | | | ka- | ma- | te | au, |
| e | | ɑu | e | | | kɑ | mɑ | te | ɑu |

| E | hi- | ne | ho- | ki | mai | ra. |
| e | hi | ne | ho | ki | maɪ | ɾɑ |

Floor   **Tap**   **Out**

McGraw-Hill School Division

Hag Shavuot
(Festival of First Fruits)

 A

Hebrew:	חַג	שָׁבוּעוֹת	בָּא זֶה הִנֵּה
Pronunciation:	xag	sha vu ot	hi ne zɛ ba
English Translation:	Holiday	weeks	Behold it's here

B

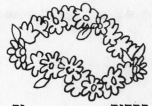

רָאשֵׁינוּ עַל
al ɾɔ she nu
On our heads

זֵר
zeɾ
garland

פְּרָחִים
pɾa xim
flowers

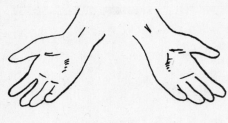

בְּיָדֵינוּ
bə ya de nu
In our hands

בִּכּוּרִים
bi ku ɾim
first fruits

English Song Text

A *Hag Shavuot, hag shavuot, hag shavuot,* the fruit is here. (*repeat*)

B We shall dress our hair with garlands, carry first fruits in our hands. (*repeat*)

Sakura
(Cherry Blossoms)

そら
so ra
sky

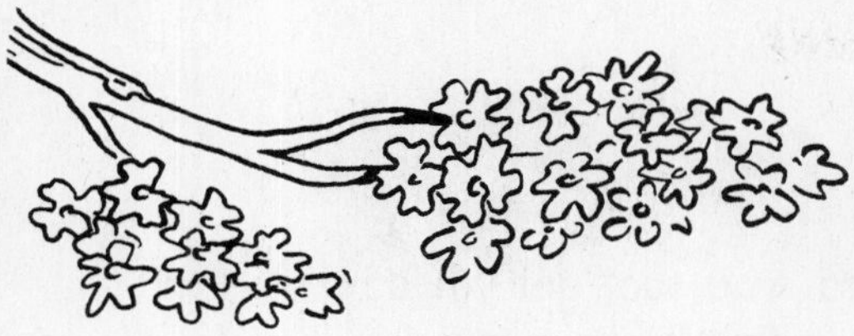

さくら
sa ku ra
cherry blossoms

におい
ni o i
fragrance

やよい
ya yo i
spring

Japanese:	さ	く	ら		さ	く	ら
Pronunciation:	**sa**	**ku**	**ra**		**sa**	**ku**	**ra**
English:	Cher-	ry	tree,		Cher-	ry	tree!

や	よ	い	の	そ	ら	は
ya	**yo**	**i**	**no**	**so**	**ra**	**wa**
Cher-	ry	blos-	soms	ev'-	ry-	where.

み	わ	た	す	か	ぎ	り
mi	**wa**	**ta**	**su**	**ka**	**gi**	**ri**
Far	as	an-	y	eye	can	see.

か	す	み	か	く	も	か
ka	**su**	**mi**	**ka**	**ku**	**mo**	**ka**
Mist	and	beau-	ty	fill	the	air,

に	お	い	ぞ	い	ず	る
ni	**o**	**i**	**zo**	**i**	**zu**	**ru**
Love-	ly	blos-	soms	scent	the	breeze.

い	ざ	や		い	ざ	や
i	**za**	**ya**		**i**	**za**	**ya**
Come	with	me,		come	with	me,

み	に	ゆ	か	ん	
mi	**ni**	**yu**	**ka**	**ṇ**	
Let	us	go	and	see.	

いざやみにゆかん
i za ya mi ni yu ka ṇ
let's go see

VISUAL AID 18 • **Song Map**

Tai Yau Tsai

(Herding the Cows)

山
san
hill

木 笛
mɔ dɑɪ
wood flute

牛
yɑʊ
cow

草 原
cho yun
meadow

Cantonese: 睇 牛 仔 技 藝 多
Pronunciation: tai yɑʊ tsai gei yai dɔ
English: Herding the cows takes much skill.

一 口 氣 爬 到 上 山 坡
yʌ hɑʊ heɪ pɑ do sʌn san bo
Taking a breath, I climb up the hill.

看 守 牛 羊 本 領 大
hɔn sɑʊ yɑʊ yən bʊn leng dɑɪ
Watching cows, what skill it takes!

木 笛 呢 吹 奏 更 柔 揚
mɔ dɑɪ lei chɔi tsɑʊ gʌng yau yʌn
I play my flute, hear the sound it makes.

睇 牛 仔 技 藝 多
tai yɑʊ tsai gei yai dɔ
Herding the cows takes much skill.

一 口 氣 爬 到 上 山 坡
yʌ hɑʊ heɪ pɑ do sʌn san bo
Taking a breath, I climb up the hill.

看 山 坡 青 青 草 原 長
han san bo tsɛng tsɛng cho yun chʌn
I see green hills, the meadow long,

看 牛 兒 羊 兒 健 又 強
han yɑʊ yi yən yi ging yau kə
I see my cows are healthy and strong.

Tai Yau Tsai
(Herding the Cows)

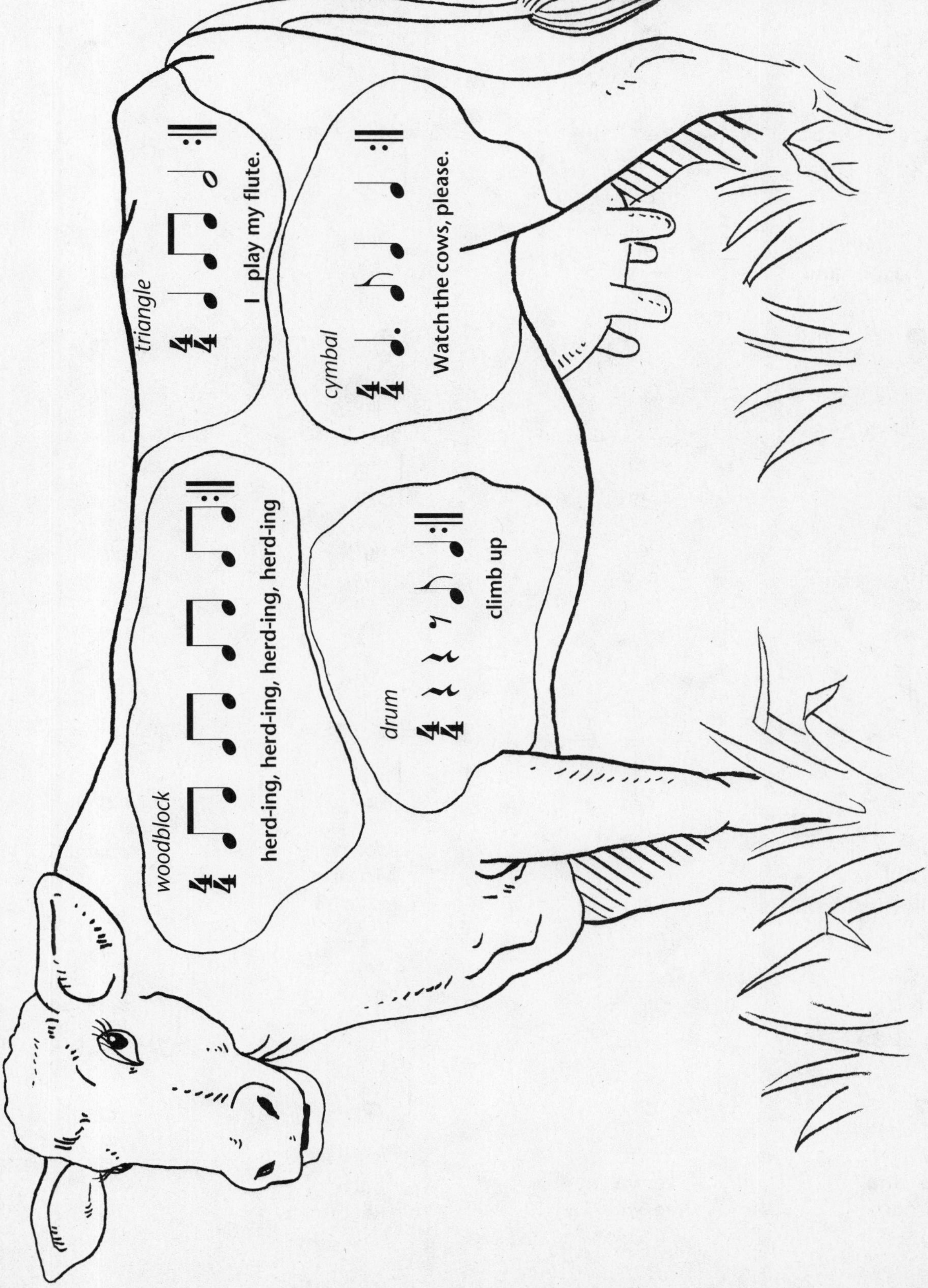

triangle

I play my flute.

cymbal

Watch the cows, please.

woodblock

herd-ing, herd-ing, herd-ing, herd-ing

drum

climb up

Hoe Ana Te Vaka
(Paddle the Canoe)

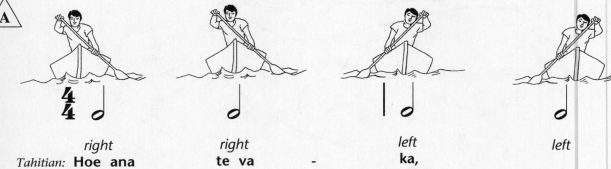

A

$\frac{4}{4}$

right
Tahitian: **Hoe ana**
Pronunciation: ho e a na

right
te va -
te va

left
ka,
ka,

left

right
Ho -
ho

left
e a -
e a

right
na,
na

left

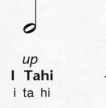 

up
I Tahi -
i ta hi

up
ti,
ti

down
Mo'ore -
mo 'o re

down
a,
a

right
Hoe ana
ho e a na

right
te va -
te va

left
ka.
ka

left

Hoe Ana Te Vaka

(Paddle the Canoe)

B

push
Ti -
ti

push
ai
a i

push
mai,
mai

push

sweep
Te
tae

sweep
Te
tae

sweep
Te
tae

sweep

wave
I -
i

wave
a o
a o

wave
e
ə

wave

tap
Ta -
ta

tap
'u he -
'u he

pat
re.
ɹə

pat

Suk San Wan Pi Mai

(New Year's Song)

Laotian: ວັນ ນີ້ ວັນ ດີ ປີ ໃໝ່ ເຮົາ ມາ ອວຍ ໄຊ ໃຫ້ ສຸກ ສຳ ລານ
Pronunciation: wan ni wan di pi mai hau ma 'uai sai hai suk sam lan
English: Today, today good New Year's Day, We wish you luck today!

ຊ່ວຍ ສ້າງ ວັນ ນີ້ ໃຫ້ ເປັນ ແດນ ສະ ຫວັນ
rɔi sang wan ni hai pɛn dɛn sa wan
Come celebrate with us,

ຊ່ວຍ ສ້າງ ວັນ ນີ້ ໃຫ້ ເປັນ ແດນ ສະ ຫວັນ
rɔi sang wan ni hai pɛn dɛn sa wan
Come celebrate with us,

ມາ ຟ້ອນ ລຳ ກັນ ສະ ຫລອງ ວັນ ປີ ໃໝ່
ma fɔn lam kan sa lɔng wan pi mai
Come celebrate a Happy New Year.

Share World Music: Songs from Asia and Oceania for Grades K–6

San Lun Tsa
(Three-Wheeled Taxi)

Measure 1

mp

Mandarin: 三 輪 車 跑 得 快
Pronunciation: sɑn luɛn chəɾ pɑu di kwɑi
English: Shall I come? Shall I go?

Measure 2

mf

上 面 坐 個 老 太 太
sɑn miɛn juɔ gəɾ lɑu tɑi tɑi
East or West I do not know!

Measure 3

p

要 五 毛 給 一 塊
yɑu wu mɑo gei yi kwɑi
I am lost all alone,

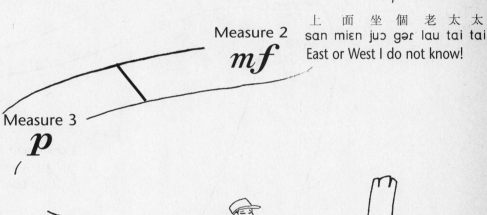

Measure 4

f

你 説 奇 怪 不 奇 怪
ni shuɔ chi gwɑi bu chi gwɑi
Three-wheeled taxi, take me home!

VISUAL AID 23 • **Song Map**

Korobushka

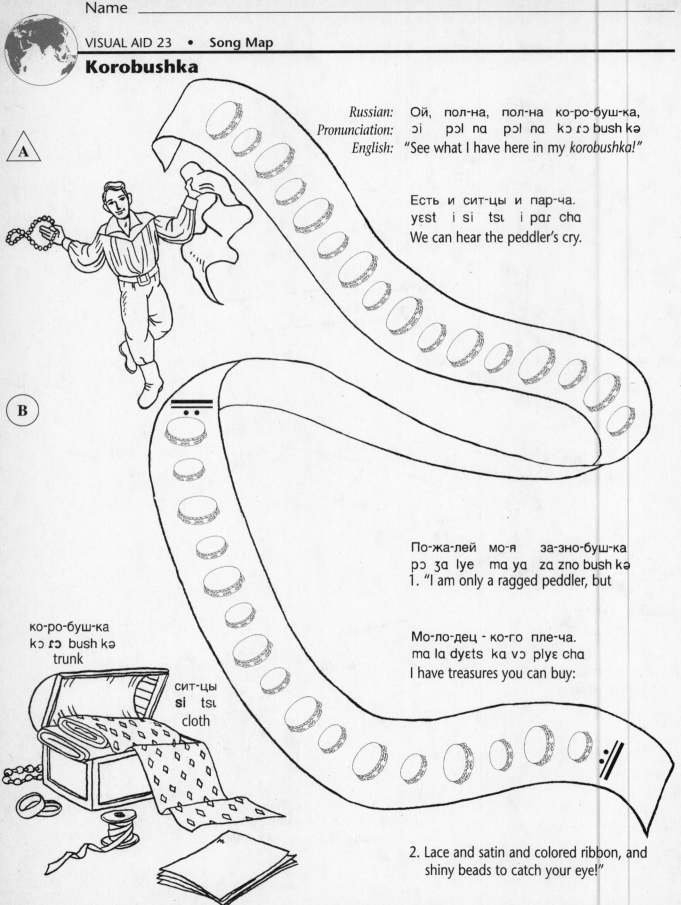

A

Russian: Ой, пол-на, пол-на ко-ро-буш-ка,
Pronunciation: ɔi ̇ pɔl na ̇ pɔl na ̇ kɔ ɾɔ bush kə
English: "See what I have here in my *korobushka!*"

Есть и сит-цы и пар-ча.
yɛst i si tsɪ i paɾ cha
We can hear the peddler's cry.

B

По-жа-лей мо-я за-зно-буш-ка
pɔ ʒa lye ̇ ma ya ̇ za zno bush kə
1. "I am only a ragged peddler, but

ко-ро-буш-ка
kɔ ɾɔ bush kə
trunk

сит-цы
si tsɪ
cloth

Мо-ло-дец - ко-го пле-ча.
ma la dyɛts ka vɔ plyɛ cha
I have treasures you can buy:

2. Lace and satin and colored ribbon, and
shiny beads to catch your eye!"

McGraw-Hill School Division

Name _____

Ua Txiab

Verse 1

	All	Solo
Hmong:	**Ua txiab niam es,**	**Ca xyoo nov es yuav mus muaj ib tug mi txiv zoo le koj os**
Pronunciation:	uwɔ tsiə niə ɛ	gyɑ yõng nɔ ɛ yuɔ mu muɔ i thu mi tsi ʒongle kˀɔ ɔ
English:	*Ua txiab niam es,*	This year I am thankful for a father like you, good father,

	All	Solo
	ntuj es os.	**Ca xyoo nov es yuav mus muaj koj los khwv zaub mov rau peb noj**
	thu ɛ ɔ	gyɑ yõng nɔ ɛ yuɔ mu muɔ kˀɔ lɔ ku ʒɑʊ mɔ dɑʊ beɪ nɔ
	ntuj es os.	This year I am thankful you provide us with food, good father,

	All
	ntuj es os.
	thu ɛ ɔ
	ntuj es os.

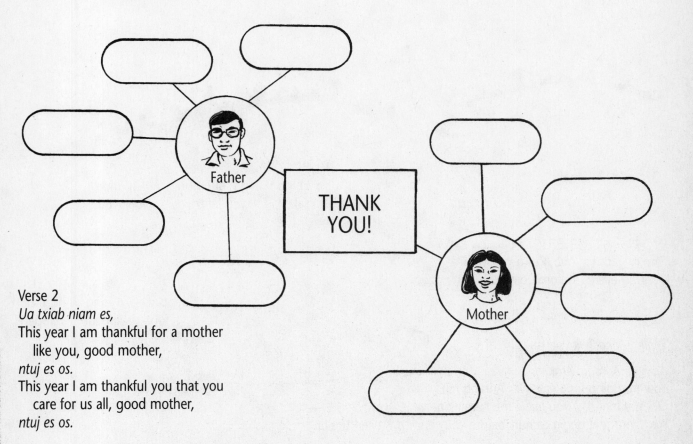

Verse 2

Ua txiab niam es,
This year I am thankful for a mother
   like you, good mother,
ntuj es os.
This year I am thankful you that you
   care for us all, good mother,
ntuj es os.

Arirang

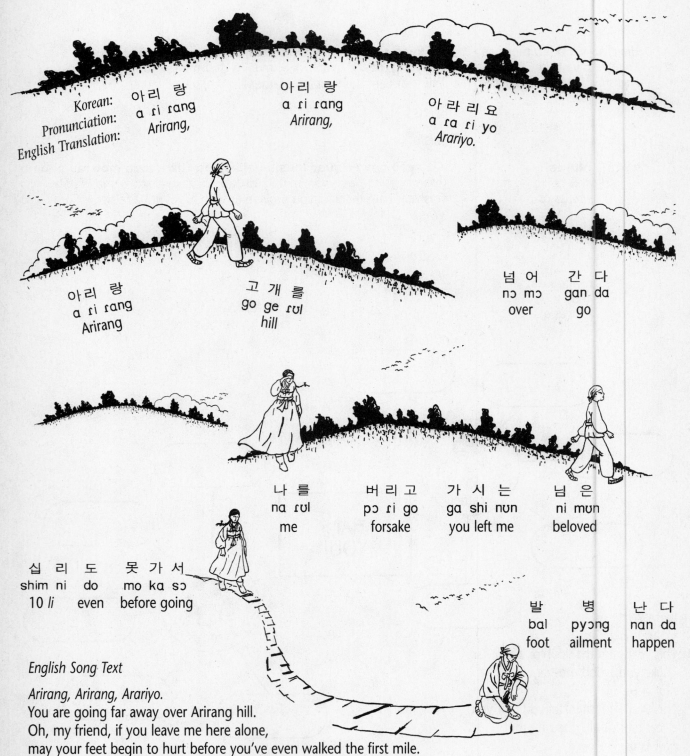

Korean: 아리 랑
Pronunciation: a ɾi ɾang
English Translation: Arirang,

아리 랑
a ɾi ɾang
Arirang,

아라리요
a ɾa ɾi yo
Arariyo.

아리 랑
a ɾi ɾang
Arirang

고 개 를
go ge ɾʉl
hill

넘 어 간 다
nʌm ʌm gan da
over go

나 를
na ɾʉl
me

버 리 고
pɔ ɾi go
forsake

가 시 는
ga shi nʉn
you left me

님 은
ni mʉn
beloved

십 리 도   못 가 서
shim ni do   mo ka sɔ
10 *li* even before going

발 병 난 다
bal pyɔng nan da
foot ailment happen

English Song Text

Arirang, Arirang, Arariyo.
You are going far away over Arirang hill.
Oh, my friend, if you leave me here alone,
may your feet begin to hurt before you've even walked the first mile.

Name _____

Tết Trung
(Children's Festival)

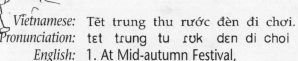

Vietnamese: Tết trung thu rước đèn đi chơi.
Pronunciation: tɛt tɾung tu ɾʊk dɛn di choi
English: 1. At Mid-autumn Festival,

Em rước đèn đi khắp phõ phường.
ɛm ɾʊk dɛn di kap fo fʊng
Walk around with lanterns lit.

Long vui sướng với đèn trong tay.
lʌng vuɪ sʊng voɪ dɛn tɾʌng taɪ
Take them all across the town,

Em múa ca trong ánh trăng rằm.
ɛm muə ka tɾʌng ʌn tɾang ɾam
Singing to the autumn moon.

Đèn ông sao với đèn cá chám.
dɛn ʌng saʊ voɪ dɛn ka cham
Lanterns all in different shapes,

Đèn thiên nga với đen bướm bướm,
dɛn tiɛn nga voɪ dɛn bʊm bʊm
Lantern angel, lantern dream,

em rước đèn này đèn cung trăng.
ɛm ɾʊk dɛn naɪ dɛn kung tɾang
Lantern fish, or lantern star,

Đèn xanh lơ với đèn tím tím.
dɛn sʌn lə voɪ dɛn tim tim
Lantern swan or butterfly.

Đèn xanh lam với đèn trắng trắng,
dɛn sʌn lam voɪ dɛn tɾang tɾang
Take my lantern to the sky;

trong ánh đèn rực rỡ muôn màu.
tɾʌng ʌn dɛn ɾʊk ɾʊ mun maʊ
Take my lantern to the moon.

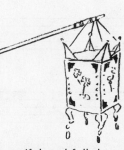

2. Beautiful and full the moon,
Waiting for the moon to rise,
Tung yin yin kak tung yin yin,
I can hear the sound of drums,
Tung yin yin kak tung yin yin.

At Mid-autumn Festival.
I can hear the sound of drums,
Tung yin yin kak tung yin yin.
Tung yin yin kak tung yin yin,
Welcome, lady in the moon!

Tết Trung
(Children's Festival)

Countermelody A

Countermelody B

Share World Music: Songs from Asia and Oceania **for Grades K–6**

Tết Trung
(Children's Festival)

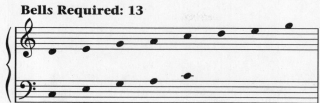

Bells Required: 13

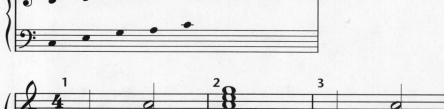

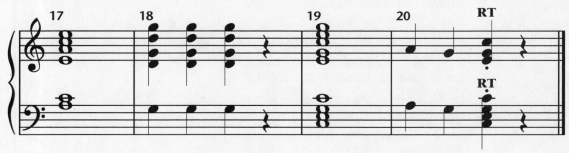

Pung Noy Loy Kratong
(Full Moon Float)

เดือน
duan
moon

ดาว
dau
stars

ลอย กระ ทง
lɔi kɾa tong
float boat

Thai: ผึ้ง น้อย ลอย กระ ทง รำ วง กัน แบบ ไทย ไทย
Pronunciation: pʊng nɔi lɔi kɾa tong ɾam wong kan bæb taɪ taɪ
English: Celebrate Loy Kratong, Oh, do the float dance.

เดือน และ ดาว ลอย เด่น เห็น จันทร์ เพ็ญ แล้ว ชื่น ใจ
duan læ dau lɔi dɛn hɛn jan pɛn læu chʊn jaɪ
When the canals are full, moon and stars are floating.

ลำ คลอง น้ำ นอง เต็ม เปี่ยม เอ่ย เรียม จะ ช้า อยู่ ใย
lam klɔng nam nɔng tem piɛm əi ɾiɛm ja cha yu yaɪ
The full moon makes us dance, *oi!* Brother, why so slow?

น้อง เอ่ย พี่ เอ่ย น้อง เอ่ย
nɔng əi pi əi nɔng əi
Brother, *oi!* Sister, *oi!* Come, *oi!*

พี่ เอ่ย มา รำ วง กัน วัน ลอย กระ ทง
pi əi ma ɾam wong kan wan lɔi kɾa tong
Let's dance and celebrate the Loy Kratong,

มา รำ วง กัน วัน ลอย กระ ทง
ma ɾam wong kan wan lɔi kɾa tong
Oh, dance on the full moon Loy Kratong.

Name _____

Hong Tsai Me Me
(Rainbow Sister)

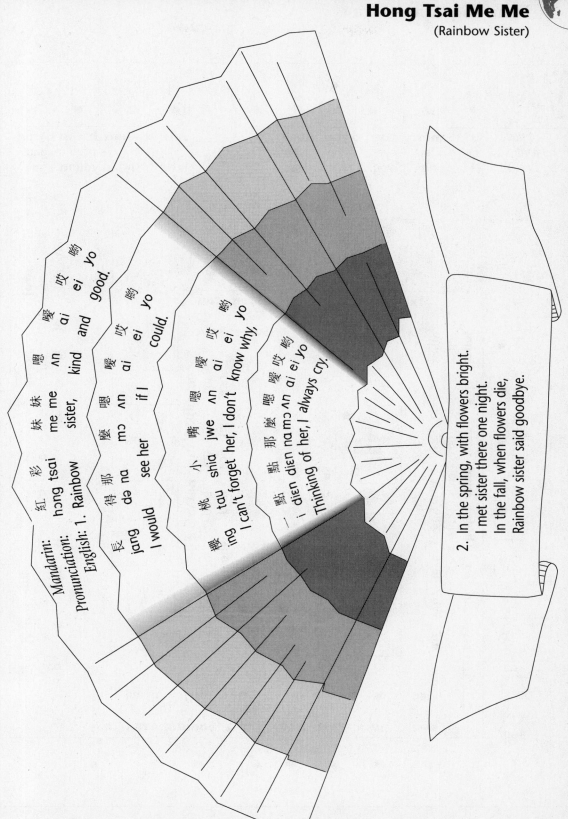

Mandarin: 紅 彩 妹 妹
Pronunciation: hɔng tsai me me
English: 1. Rainbow sister,

嗳 哎 哟
ai ei yo
kind and good.

得 那 嗳 哎 哟
jang au ep ai ei yo
I would see her if I could.

長 au cw
ing

小 嘴 嗳 哎 哟
tau shia jwe An ai ei yo
I can't forget her, I don't know why,

桃 櫻

— dien dien nɑ mɔ n ai ei yo
點 那 嗳 哎
點 那麼 嗳哎哟
Thinking of her, I always cry.

2. In the spring, with flowers bright.
I met sister there one night.
In the fall, when flowers die,
Rainbow sister said goodbye.

Nim Yog Xyoo Nuav
(In This Year)

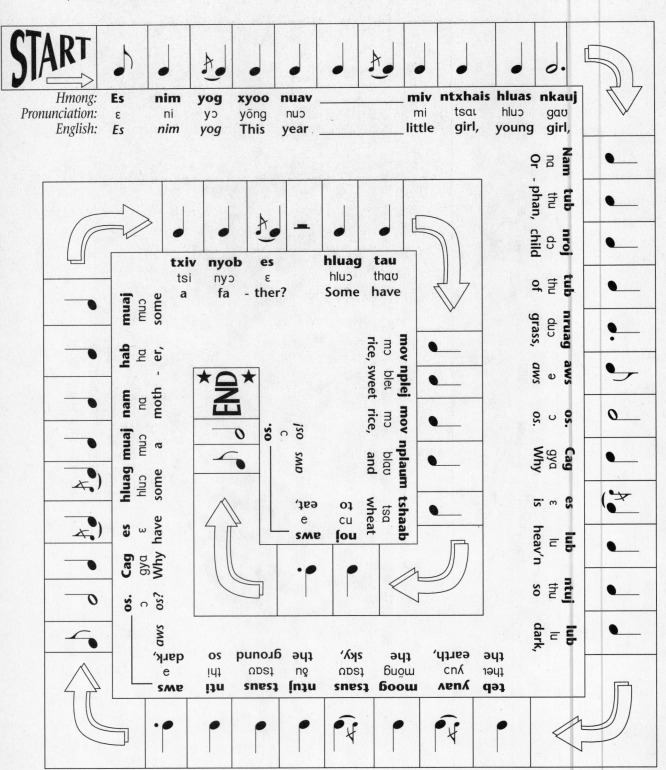

Share World Music: Songs from Asia and Oceania for Grades K–6

Name _____

Fung Yang Song

drum

4/4

Chinese: 左　　手　　鑼　　　右　　于　　鼓
Pronunciation: juɔ　shou　luɔ　　yu　shou　gu
English: **Sing the Fung Yang song.　Sing it loud and long.**

手　拿　　鑼　鼓　來　唱　歌
shou　na　　luɔ　gu　lai　chang　gə
With drums and cym-bals we　sing the Fung Yang song.

別　的　　歌　兒　我　也　不　會　唱
biɛ　di　　gə　ər　wɔ　yɛ　bu　hwe　chang
This　is　a song　we can　sing the whole day long.

只　會　　唱　個　鳳　陽　歌
jə　hwe　　chang　gə　fʌng　yang　gə
We　strike　the gong　to the Fung　Yang　song.

B

鳳　陽　歌　來　依　呵　呀
fʌng　yang　gə　lai　yi　ho　ya
Flower drums of Fung Yang, yi ho ya,

得兒　鈴　鐺　瓢　一　瓢　得兒　鈴　鐺　瓢　一　瓢
dər　ling　tang　piao　yi　piao　dər　ling　tang　piao　yi　piao
drr ling tang piao yi piao, drr ling tang piao yi piao,

得兒　瓢　得兒　瓢　得兒　瓢　得兒　瓢　瓢　得兒瓢　鈴　鐺　瓢　一　瓢
dər piao　dər piao　dər piao　dər piao　piao dər piao　ling　tang　piao　yi　piao
drr piao, drr piao, drr piao drr piao　piao drr piao ling tang piao yi piao.

鳳
fʌng
Fung

陽
yang
Yang

歌
gə
song

左
juɔ
left

右
yu
right

手
shou
hand

鑼
luɔ
gong

鼓
gu
small drum

Üsküdar

A

Turkish: Üs - kü - dar' - a gi - der - i - ken

Pronunciation: üs kü dɑɾ ɑ gi dɛɾ i kɛn

English: Üs - kü - dar, a dis - tant __ cit - y.

al - dı - da bir yağ - mur,

ɑl di dɑ biɾ yɑ muɾ

I walk a - long the road.

B

Kâ - ti - bi - min se - tre - si u - zun

kɑ ti bi min sɛ tɾɛ si u zun

On a rain - y morn - ing _____

e - te - ği __ ça - mur.

ɛ tɛ gi jɑ muɾ

there __ I __ met __ my __ friend.

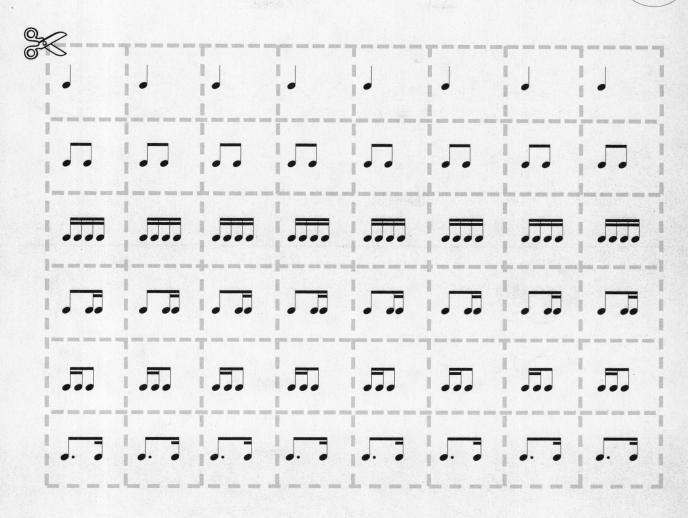

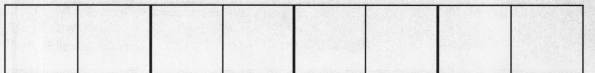

Diwali Song

A

  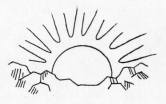 

Hindi: दी प	ज ला ओ	आ ज	दी वा ली रे
Pronunciation: di pə	ja ɖa o	ɑ jə	di wɑ li ɾe
English Translation: clay oil lamp	light them up	today	Diwali Festival

B

स ब
sɑ vɑ
all of you

हँ स ते
hã sə te
smiling

आ ओ
ɑo
come

खु शी
ku shi
happy

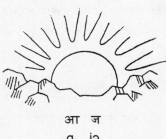

आ ज
ɑ jə
today

दी वा ली रे
di wɑ li ɾe
Diwali Festival

English Song Text

A Light up your lamps, come light them today, the day of Diwali Re.
(repeat line)

B Ev'ryone smiling and happy, Ah-oh. Today, Diwali Re. *(repeat line)*
Today, Diwali, today, Diwali, today, Diwali Re.

(Repeat A section)

Name _____

Name _____

Niam Es

A

Hmong: **Niam es, Ca xyoo nov es lub paj thawg paj twawm txi txiv os.**

Pronunciation:

English: *Niam es,* This year on the flower there's a little bud, Oh.

B

Ca xyoo nov es txiv leej tub tuaj txog rabteb mi nroj tug no
gya yõng nɔ ɛ tsi leng thu thuɔ tsɔ dɑ theɪ mi dɔ ðu nɔ
This year comes a man along the pathway before the grass grows.

es niam kho siab ua luaj li no os.
ɛ ni kɔ shiə uɔ luɔ li nɔ ɛ
He stands with a heart so sad, Oh.

tub
thu
man

A

(repeat section A)

C

Ca muaj mi kab mi noog los noj es xyoo nov es txiv
gya muɔ mi kˈa mi nõng lɔ nɔ ɛ yõng nɔ ɛ tsi
Little insects and birds come feed. This year comes a

leej tub tuaj txog ram rabteb mi nroj tug no
leng thu thuɔ tsɔ dɑ dɑ theɪ mi dɔ thu nɔ
man along the pathway before the grass grows.

es tsi muaj kuv mi nkauj hmoob los nrog nyob os mog.
ɛ tsi muɔ kˈu mi gɑʊ mõng lɔ dɔ nyɔ ɔ mɔ
Come my lovely one, Oh, come and marry me.

nkauj
gɑʊ
girl

noog
nõng
birds

A

(repeat section A)

110

Share World Music: Songs from Asia and Oceania **for Grades K–6**

McGraw-Hill School Division

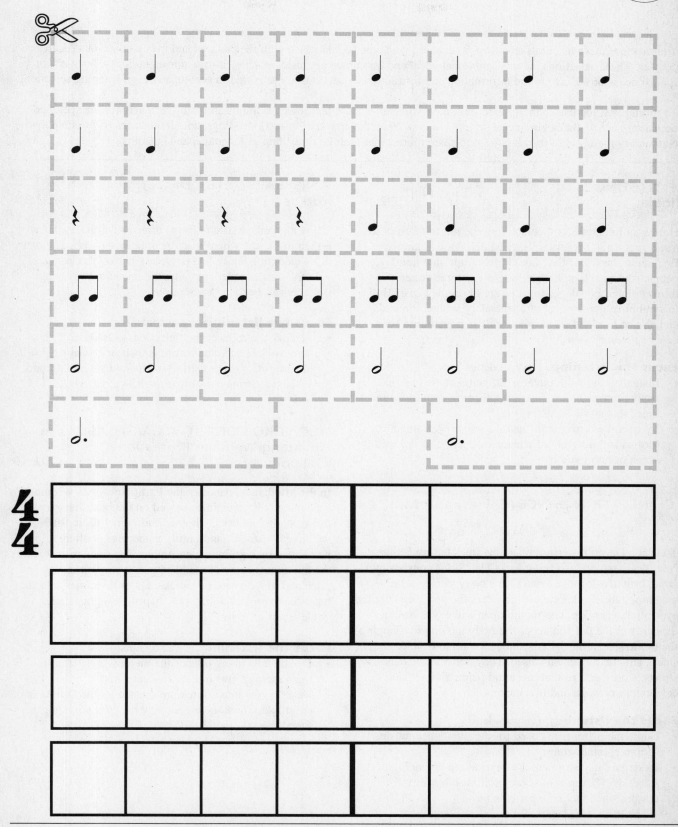

Listening Library

You may use these listening selections to enhance students' acquaintance with the cultures and music of various Asian peoples. These selections include traditional vocal and instrumental music, much of it used during holidays, festivals, or special occasions. Background information and instructional questions are provided to accompany each listening selection.

To further develop use of these selections, have students discuss their own traditions and familiar music for the specified occasions such as the beginning of spring, the New Year, the arrival of guests, weddings, and graduations. If possible, invite community members to the classroom to share more about their cultures' music, language, and customs.

HOLI SONG
India   CD2:16

Holi is an Indian festival celebrating the return of color to trees, grass, and flowers in early March. Holi is known in English as the Color Festival. On this important holiday, people squirt each other with brightly colored water and throw colored powders. Bonfires are lit on the eve of Holi to symbolize the survival of a legendary prince, Prahlad, and also to burn old household items in preparation for a new beginning in spring.

Focus the listening. Have students:
*   Listen for the three pitches that go up at the end of many phrases in this song. Ask them to count how many times this motif occurs. (7)
*   Discuss the instruments that accompany the singer. (drums and a keyboard wind instrument called a reed organ or harmonium)

CHINESE LION DANCE (Chinese Folk Music)
China   CD2:17

The Lion Dance is performed many times during Chinese New Year festivities to bring luck. The "lion" consists of a large, brightly decorated mask on a boxy frame and a matching fabric tail. One dancer wears the head, making the eyes blink, ears flap, and mouth open and close. Another dancer is in the tail and keeps the body moving by flapping the fabric sides. Martial arts students train to develop the sharp, athletic movements used. They perform the dance in streets, stores, and restaurants amid percussion music, celebratory crowds, and firecrackers.

Focus the listening. Have students:
*   Name the instruments used for the lion dance music. (drum, cymbal, gong)
*   Describe the instrumental sounds at the beginning of the selection. (Several rolls, each followed by several crashes; then the main patterns begin.)

KARŞI BAR (Turkish Dance)
Turkey   CD2:18

This folk dance music is from eastern Anatolia, a plateau region in Turkey where many people herd sheep. The dance is a welcoming dance and is usually performed in a line, with the dance leader signaling the musicians to change rhythms and begin a new section.

Focus the listening. Have students:
*   Identify the form of this selection. (ABABAB)
*   Name or describe the instruments heard. (drum, tambourine, plucked string instrument such as an oud, strummed string instrument such as a zither)

ADONGKO DONGKO A GAKIT (Philippine Kulintang Wedding Processional)
Philippines   CD2:19

In the Mindanao Islands of the Philippines, this wedding processional is sometimes played on the boat that carries the groom to the bride's home. Philippine music for weddings, festivals, and family gatherings is often performed by a kulintang ensemble. The main instrument is the kulintang, a row of knobbed gongs varying in size and pitch and played with two sticks. Other instruments include hand-held gongs, hanging pot-shaped bass gongs, and goblet-shaped drums.

Focus the listening. Have students:
*   Decide how many pitches the melody uses. (four in the main melody, five in later restatements)
*   Describe the musical texture created by the kulintang ensemble. (thick, layered, many rhythms sounding together)

TSING CHUN U CHÜ (Youth Dance Song)
Taiwan   CD2:20

This song is sung as a goodbye to youth by students and teenagers in Taiwan. Taiwan is a large island off the east coast of China, and many people living there are Chinese immigrants and their descendants. This song was brought to Taiwan from China and may have originally come from the Uigur, a Turkic people of northwestern China known for lively music and dance.

Focus the listening. Have students:
- Tell whether this song is in major or minor. (minor)
- Discuss how the lyrics suggest a farewell. (Final repeated idea is that some things, once gone, never return.)

BO HAI HUAN TEN
China   CD2:21

The title of this Chinese New Year music means "Jubilation All Around" in English. Traditional Chinese orchestras such as the one playing this selection include plucked, bowed, and hammered string instruments; reed instruments and flutes; and gongs, cymbals, and drums.

Focus the listening. Have students:
- Name the instrument families represented in this recording. (strings, woodwinds, percussion; no brass)
- Count how many times the percussion instruments are heard by themselves. (5)

HAJI FIRUZ
Iran   CD2:22

People from Iran celebrate the New Year on the first day of spring. The thirteen-day celebration is called Noruz and includes singing and dancing, gift giving, and visiting. At family picnics, entertainers such as clowns and acrobats are part of the fun. One of the entertainers' roles is Haji Firuz, a man in baggy red clothing and a cone-shaped hat who plays the tambourine.

Focus the listening. Have students:
- Describe the instruments heard in the accompaniment. (hammered dulcimer, drum)
- Describe the melodic direction of the sequence heard in the interlude. (downward)

A Musical Sound Tour

The following narrative can be used for class or individual instruction.
- Read, or have a student read, the narrative, pausing and playing each sound example.
- Have a photocopy of the narrative, together with the compact disc, available in a learning center for students to read and listen to individually.
- Distribute copies of the map (page 118) for students to follow as they listen to the sound tour. As the tour proceeds, students can draw their route on the map by locating each new area and connecting it to the previous one with a line.

1. Join us in a sound tour to hear some of the many musical instruments of the world. Our first stop will be Turkey, where you will hear the sound of the **saz** (saz), an instrument popular in many Balkan and southwest Asian countries. Known as the "long lute of Turkey," the saz comes in a range of sizes up to five feet long.

   It is a lute, a stringed instrument with a body that is the shape of a pear half. The saz has three pairs of strings (each pitch sounds on two strings) and movable frets of gut tied around the neck. A saz player plucks the strings with a hide plectrum, or pick. **(CD2:23)**

2. Next, listen to the sound of the **dumbek** (dum bɛk), a type of drum known as a goblet drum because of its drinking glass shape. The base of the dumbek is made of wood, clay, or metal, and it is often decorated with elaborate designs. The player performs rhythms on the dumbek using both hands. **(CD2:24)**

3. Traveling east, let's stop in Iran to hear a **santur** (san tur). This instrument is a type of hammered dulcimer, or board zither. The santur's metal strings run along the length of a trapezoidal sound box. There are usually three strings per note. The player strikes the strings with small wooden hammers. **(CD2:25)**

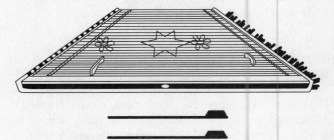

4. The music of northern India uses a variety of string and percussion instruments. Let's first hear the **sitar** (sɪ tar or sɪ tar), a solo instrument that is a long-necked lute. The sitar has a gourd sound box and is equipped with a second sound box, or resonator, behind the neck. The sitar has two sets of strings that run parallel to each other. Using a stiff wire plectrum, the player plucks the top set of strings, producing both melody and drone. The bottom set of strings vibrate when the top set is played. **(CD2:26)**

McGraw-Hill School Division

5. The sitar is often part of a performing group that includes the **tabla** (tɑ blɑ). Tabla are always played in pairs. The left-hand drum is bowl-shaped and is usually metal. The right-hand drum is cylinder-shaped and is made of wood. Both drums are tuned. The player sits cross-legged and plays intricate *tala*, or rhythmic sets, with the fingertips, palms, and heels of the hand. **(CD2:27)**

6. Traveling still further east, let's hear four traditional Chinese musical instruments. The **zheng** (chʌng) is a long zither. The zheng, which dates from around 900 B.C., is still popular. Today, most zhengs have 16 or 21 strings. The player kneels or sits cross-legged in front of the instrument, plucking the strings. Many ornaments and variations of tone color can be created by pressing and pulling on the individual strings. **(CD2:28)**

7. The **dizi** (di tsə) is a Chinese flute made of bamboo. One of the holes near the top of the dizi is covered with a thin sheet of bamboo paper. This vibrates to give a slightly reedy quality to the tone. The player holds the flute to the right in a position similar to the Western orchestral flute. **(CD2:29)**

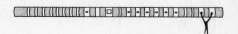

8. The **erhu** (ɛr hu) is a two-string fiddle. It has a small, six- or eight-sided resonating chamber and a long neck. The player holds the erhu in his or her lap and places the bow between the strings, playing only one string at a time. The strings are stopped with finger pressure alone since the instrument does not have a fingerboard. **(CD2:30)**

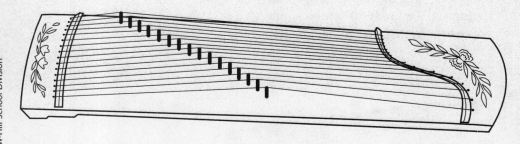

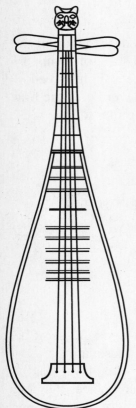

9. The **p'i-p'a** (pǐ pɑ) is a lute with four strings. Frets extending down onto the body of the instrument guide the player, who produces a wide range of performance effects through skillful plucking. **(CD2:31)**

10. Traveling on to Japan, let's hear the sound of the **shakuhachi** (shɑ ku hɑ chǐ), another bamboo flute. It is popular as an ensemble instrument. The shakuhachi has four finger holes and one thumb hole which produce a pentatonic scale. The player blows into it from the end to produce haunting, expressive sounds. **(CD2:32)**

11. The **koto** (kǒ to) is a Japanese zither, usually with 13 strings. Each string is supported by its own moveable bridge, enabling the player to easily adjust the tuning. The koto's strings are plucked with a plectrum. A skilled player can create many ornaments and changes of tone color. Today, the instrument is widely played both as an important part of traditional Japanese ensembles, and as a popular solo instrument. **(CD2:33)**

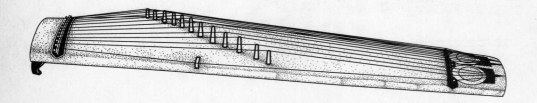

12. The Philippines are the home of the **kulintang** (ku lɪn tɑng), a set of 8 to 11 knobbed pot-shaped gongs placed on a rack. These pitched bronze gongs are struck with wooden mallets. The kulintang is the melody instrument of the ensemble that is also called "kulintang." This all-percussion group is made up entirely of gongs and drums. **(CD2:34)**

13. Our last stop is Tahiti, where we can hear the sounds of the **tōʼere** (to ʼe ɾe), a drum made from a slit log and played with two wooden beaters. The tōʼere is often used to accompany dancing. **(CD2:35)**

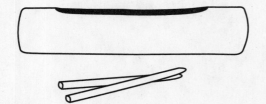

14. The **ʼukulele** (ʼu ku le le or yu kə leɪ li) is another popular instrument of Tahiti. (The first pronunciation is used in Hawaii, the second is Americanized.) It is a small guitar with four strings. The ʼukulele came to Tahiti from Hawaii, where it was developed about 150 years ago. This relative newcomer frequently accompanies song and dance throughout Oceania. **(CD2:36)**

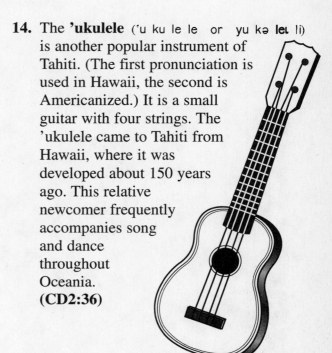

Share World Music: Songs from Asia and Oceania for Grades K–6

McGraw-Hill School Division

ACTIVITIES

Classifying Musical Instruments

There are many ways to classify musical instruments. Have students play the role of an ethnomusicologist (a music specialist who studies folk and traditional music in various cultures) and compare the three lutes shown in the musical tour (the saz, the sitar, and the p'i-p'a). Describe such things as the shape of the instrument body, the length of the neck relative to the body, the number of strings, the presence or absence of frets, and the location and appearance of the tuning pegs.

Community Connection

Arrange for students to visit an art museum and look for representations of musical instruments in painting and sculpture. See if any of the instruments resemble those in the Sound Tour. (Hint: look for angel choirs in paintings done around 1400. These frequently show lutes, dulcimers, and harps. Asian paintings often show musicians and instruments in court scenes.) If a museum is not close by, visit the library and look for reproductions in art history books. Students should take note of their findings and bring them back to class for discussion and comparison.

ALPHABETICAL LISTING OF INSTRUMENTS

dizi (China) **CD2:29**
dumbek (Turkey) **CD2:24**
erhu (China) **CD2:30**
koto (Japan) **CD2:33**
kulintang (Philippines) **CD2:34**
p'i-p'a (China) **CD2:31**
santur (Iran) **CD2:25**
saz (Turkey) **CD2:23**
shakuhachi (Japan) **CD2:32**
sitar (India) **CD2:26**
tabla (India) **CD2:27**
tō'ere (Tahiti) **CD2:35**
'ukulele (Tahiti) **CD2:36**
zheng (China) **CD2:28**

ARE YOU CULTURALLY SENSITIVE?

Use the following informal checklist to assess your cultural sensitivity.

CLASSROOM ATMOSPHERE

Yes	Sometimes	No	
☐	☐	☐	• Do you discuss your own cultural heritage with students?
☐	☐	☐	• Do you know the cultural backgrounds of your students?
☐	☐	☐	• Are you interested in knowing how your students' cultural backgrounds influence their values, beliefs, and understanding of the world?
☐	☐	☐	• Do you let your students teach you what you don't understand about their cultures?
☐	☐	☐	• Do you discuss with students the impact that culture has on our lives?
☐	☐	☐	• Do you work to clarify misconceptions, negative beliefs, and stereotypes about people from diverse cultures, ethnic groups, and religions?
☐	☐	☐	• Are you aware of your own stereotypes?
☐	☐	☐	• Do you guard against letting your stereotypes interfere with your students' growth?

CLASSROOM CONTENT AND INSTRUCTION

Yes	Sometimes	No	
☐	☐	☐	• Do you consider that students with different cultural backgrounds may have different learning styles and may respond to some approaches better than others?
☐	☐	☐	• Do you use assessment techniques that allow for a variety of learning styles?
☐	☐	☐	• Do you help students view events and issues from a variety of perspectives?
☐	☐	☐	• Do you encourage students to explore various perspectives when thinking through an issue or problem?
☐	☐	☐	• Do you review classroom materials for cultural sensitivity and accuracy?
☐	☐	☐	• Do you provide reading materials by and about people from diverse backgrounds?
☐	☐	☐	• Is multiculturalism central to your language arts, social studies, and arts content/instruction rather than simply added on or addressed from time to time?

STUDENTS ACQUIRING A SECOND LANGUAGE

Overview

A popular misconception regarding multicultural education is that it is intended primarily or exclusively for minority students. . . . Because all students ultimately will need to function in our culturally diverse society, all should be exposed to educational experiences that foster the necessary competencies for doing so.

Students are likely to learn best in instructional environments that are consistent with their learning-style preferences. For this reason, teachers faced with culturally diverse classes and students who differ in their learning preferences must be able to draw upon a variety of teaching strategies appropriate to various learning styles. (Hernández, Hilda. Multicultural Education: A Teacher's Guide to Content and Processes. Columbus, Ohio: Merrill, 1989.)

Q
A
How do I help a student acquire a second language?

- Use a lot of repetition. Say and do things many times in one class period and on subsequent days.
- Present your lesson in small "chunks" of information. Progress from easy to more difficult in small increments. For example, have students sing just the repeated phrase of a song before asking them to sing the entire chorus. Then have them begin learning a verse.
- Select concepts and vocabulary that you want every student to master, and give those items increased emphasis by using repetition. Target two or three key words in each lesson. Work primarily toward helping students to start singing and secondarily toward giving them an idea of the content.
- Acknowledge and praise or validate all student responses.

Q
A
What are some techniques for presenting information to students acquiring a second language?

- Use a variety of teaching approaches in order to include all learning styles. Include small-group, large-group, aural, kinesthetic, and visual activities in your lesson.
- Use silent signal directions when possible.
- Act out words and emphasize meaning with your voice. Use movement to bring meaning to words whenever possible. Ham it up! (examples: Clap on accented syllables; raise arms in air for high; and so on.)
- Use visuals that have both pictures and words. Point to appropriate pictures as you go along.
- Use other school materials and resources such as library books, videos, and Web sites to aid the students in acquiring more background information on the vocabulary or song.
- Speak and give directions at a slower tempo than you would for single-language classes. Use a clear, slow speaking voice in a high or medium range, avoiding a monotone or low speaking range. Keep sentences relatively short and simple. Sing directions whenever possible to add musical interest and to encourage listening.
- Ask single-response questions that can be answered with *yes, no,* or another one-word answer to provide opportunities for success.

**Q
A**

How do I accommodate language differences in my classroom?

- Seat a student acquiring a second language next to a native speaker to provide a good role model and a "buddy."
- Have students follow with their fingers when using a textbook or an individual copy of a song map. (example: On a song map, have them point to the picture that represents each phrase while singing that phrase.)
- Summarize material periodically throughout the lesson and relate it to the objective of the lesson.
- Elaborate on what the student acquiring a second language says by restating and adding additional meaning and information.
- Make meaning a priority; pronunciation and sentence structure will improve in due course.
- Have the same expectations for students who are acquiring a second language that you have for your native speakers. When provided with adequate instruction, their skill development should be equal to that of their peers. The only exception to this is when language is a barrier to their being able to tell you what they have learned. Leveling down for students who are acquiring a second language is an inappropriate teaching technique.

**Q
A**

How do I work to improve students' production of sounds and words?

- Listen to students' diction as well as to rhythmic and melodic accuracy, intonation, and other aspects of musicality. Correct diction when appropriate by rephrasing or repeating the problem words or sounds.
- Watch for students who exhibit difficulty with aural discrimination. Students who mispronounce words may not be hearing them correctly.
- Set up a listening center in which students may listen to and practice with recorded pronunciations and songs.
- Allow students ample time to pronounce the words in the context of the lesson. Use the words in the rhythmic context of the song.
- Use the recording while pointing to the vocabulary words on the board.
- Have native speakers lead students acquiring a second language in saying the words.
- Remind students to look at your mouth for the pronunciation of difficult words.
- Avoid overdoing pronunciation practice. Limit to about three the number of times students practice the words and let the song teach the words.

**Q
A**

How can I help promote a sense of positive self-esteem and belonging for students acquiring a second language?

- Plan a review of familiar material for every music lesson (a song or a movement activity with which students are comfortable). This provides students with a sense of security and success. Structure your lessons around a routine that students will become familiar with.

Share World Music: Songs from Asia and Oceania **for Grades K–6**

- Show respect for the students' native languages by pronouncing names correctly.
- Use greetings with unchanging texts. (example: Good day, everyone.)
- Assign classroom duties to the student acquiring a second language to increase involvement and responsibility. (examples: page turner, material distributor/collector)
- Sing songs in a language unfamiliar to all, or use sign language, thus putting all students on equal experience and ability levels.
- Learn about the non-native speakers' cultures and show respect for them by including information on them in your lessons. Promote cultural diversity by making it a part of your lessons and challenging students to learn about each other and about cultures not represented in their class.
- Acknowledge and praise student responses and participation.

SHARE WORLD MUSIC LESSONS

Q
A
How much time do I spend teaching the songs?

- Allow more than one class period to work on learning the vocabulary words and the song before teaching the lesson objective.

Q
A
How do I help students learn the songs?

- Have students listen to the entire recording before they learn the song.
- Sing the song at a slower tempo than the recording to allow students time to practice using their new vocabulary. After two or three tries at the slower tempo, challenge students to sing the song up to tempo with the recording. If needed, slow the tempo again, then try the faster tempo after two more tries.
- Separate the melody from the words by using vocalises to correct problems. (example: Sing on *la* or *loo,* or hum the song.)
- Preview song maps with students, noting where the song begins (not always at the top), key words and pictures, and where the song ends, as well as the title of the song.

Q
A
What are some ways to teach key vocabulary?

- Provide students with frequent opportunities to see and hear the words. Frequent repetition and practice will aid them in learning the words.
- List all vocabulary words on the board using large letters so they can be read from the back of the room. Use care with handwriting. Avoid mixing lowercase and uppercase letters.
- Use color on the chalkboard to stimulate interest.
- When possible, use pictures with the vocabulary words.
- Use voice inflection to emphasize words and syllables. Add movements or pantomime to emphasize the meaning of the words.

- Echo-say the song, first with the teacher as the leader, then with a student as the leader. (Choose a student leader who is a native speaker.)
- Introduce the words a few at a time in the context of the song. Associate the vocabulary with objects and materials in the classroom and experiences in the students' lives.
- Make vocabulary-word charts to display for each lesson as needed.
- Put the vocabulary words and song maps in a listening station for students to review and practice with the recording. Include hand puppets and visuals as a way to help students practice saying the words or singing the song.

Q
A
What are some techniques for having students practice vocabulary?

- Allow students time to pronounce the words several times, especially on their first exposure.
- Set up a center with a tape recorder and blank tape for students to record themselves practicing vocabulary words.
- Use vocabulary flashcards in whole- or small-group settings for students to practice saying and singing song words.
- Use varying vocabulary-pronunciation practices, such as recitations, skits, dramas, group practice, and individual practices.

Q
A
When a lesson calls for small-group work, what do I do to involve all members of the group?

- Provide a time line to aid groups in staying on task and not lingering too long on any given step in the assignment. As students work, give time reminders as to where they should be.
- Assign everyone a job. (examples: writer, timekeeper, encourager, moderator, spokesperson)

Q
A
How can I modify assessment procedures to insure an accurate measurement of the knowledge of students acquiring a second language?

- Practice the assessment activity as a class before giving it individually.
- On a performance assessment, seat the student acquiring a second language near the teacher or a reliable, bilingual student who can give key words in the second language on how to complete the requirements. (examples: when to play the instrument, when to sing, and so on)
- When assessing, be sensitive to questions or instructions that present barriers to students acquiring a second language; however, learning expectations should be the same for all students.
- Address a variety of learning styles when assessing learning. Include visual, aural, and kinesthetic response opportunities.

USING VISUAL AIDS

Q
A
How can I use color to enhance my use of transparencies with students acquiring a second language?

- Use color to highlight form. (examples: A section = red; B section = blue)
- Use color to mark same/different phrases and/or melodies.
- Use color to highlight dynamics and other musical controls.
- Use color to add interest, to highlight key vocabulary words, and to illustrate words. (examples: sun = yellow; heart = red)
- Color song titles to highlight them.
- Use *erasable* transparency markers when you are having each class give input that will be marked directly on a transparency.
- Use *permanent* markers for adding color that you will use as a part of every lesson and for coloring items you will not need to change from class to class.
- Use *erasable* markers on the front side of a transparency; use permanent markers on the back side, as some transparency print will smear when colored over.

Q
A
How can I make most effective use of the overhead projector?

- If possible, leave the lights on. Most overhead projectors are designed to be used without having the room darkened.
- Use a pointer such as a beverage stirrer or pen with a cap on to follow the song map or direct students to a particular item on a transparency.
- Make sure students can see around you and around/over the projector when you are at the projector.
- Check the focus and positioning of the transparency on the screen frequently.
- Have the screen at an appropriate level for students—too high, near the ceiling, will cause them discomfort; too low will block the view of some students.
- When teaching a song from an overhead, use a sheet of paper to cover lines of words or phrases that have not yet been introduced. Slowly reveal the other lines to allow students to focus on small segments at a time.
- After using a transparency, provide copies for student review. Have students point to the pictures and/or words as they sing.

McGraw-Hill School Division

CLASSROOM INSTRUCTIONS

The following instructions are translated into four common languages currently found in classrooms with large numbers of multilingual students: Cambodian (Khmer), Cantonese, Hmong, and Vietnamese. Accompanying recorded pronunciation guides provide support in communicating effectively with students acquiring English.

To facilitate teaching students with diverse language backgrounds, you may want to learn the non-English phrases for the instructions you use most often. Adjusting the balance on your stereo so that only the non-English phrases are heard allows you time to repeat each phrase after the native speaker. Another option is to play the recordings of selected phrases in class as they are needed. Students might also listen individually to the recordings to learn the English phrases.

Instructional Phrases	ENGLISH	CAMBODIAN (KHMER)
CD2:37	Did the melody go up, go down, or stay the same?	តើសំលេងទ្បើង ឬចុះ ឬនៅដដែល?
	Do what I do.	ធ្វើតាមខ្ញុំ
	Don't talk.	កុំនិយាយ
	Echo back.	ថាតាមខ្ញុំ
CD2:38	Form a line.	តំរង់ជួរ
	Form a circle.	ធ្វើរង្វង់
	Go get _____.	ទៅយក ____
	groups	ក្រុម
	Divide into groups.	បំបែកជាក្រុម
CD2:39	How does this sound?	សំលេងនេះយ៉ាងម៉េចទៅ?
	Listen carefully.	ស្ដាប់ឱ្យបានល្អ
	Look at me.	មើលមកខ្ញុំ
	Make this sound.	ធ្វើសំលេងនេះ
	March in a circle.	ដើរជារង្វង់
CD2:40	partners	ដៃគូ
	Change partners.	ផ្លាស់ដៃគូ
	Face your partner.	សម្លឹងដៃគូ
	Select a partner.	រើសដៃគូ
	Pick it up.	រើសវាឡើង
	Put your hands in your lap.	ដាក់ដៃលើភ្លៅ
CD2:41	Raise your hand.	លើកដៃឡើង
	Raise your hand before speaking.	លើកដៃមុននិយាយ
	ready	ត្រៀមខ្លួន
	Ready, begin.	ត្រៀមខ្លួន ចាប់ផ្ដើម
	Ready, move.	ត្រៀមខ្លួន ទៅ
	Ready, play.	ត្រៀមខ្លួន លេង
	Ready, sing.	ត្រៀមខ្លួន ច្រៀង
CD2:42	Stand side by side.	ឈរ ទល់មុខគ្នា
	This is called _____.	នេះហៅថា ____
	Turn and face me.	បែរមុខមកខ្ញុំ

Share World Music: Songs from Asia and Oceania for Grades K–6

Instructional Words	ENGLISH	CAMBODIAN (KHMER)
CD2:43	begin	ចាប់ផ្ដើម
	bow	អោន
	clap	ទះដៃ
	conduct	ដឹកនាំ
	different	ផ្សេង
CD 2:44	enter	ចូល
	left hand	ឆ្វេងដៃ
	to the left	ខាងឆ្វេង
	listen	ស្ដាប់
	pat	ស្ទាប
	move	ផ្លើចលនា
CD2:45	read	អាន
	return	ត្រឡប់មកវិញ
	right hand	ដៃស្ដាំ
	to the right	ខាងស្ដាំដៃ
	say	និយាយ
	show me	បង្ហាញខ្ញុំ
CD2:46	sing	ច្រៀង
	speak	និយាយ
	think	គិត
	wait	ចាំ
	whisper	ខ្សិប
	write	សរសេរ

Greetings and Courtesies

CD2:47	Excuse me.	សូមទោស
	Goodbye.	លាហើយ
	Good try.	ល្អណាស់
	Happy birthday!	ជូនពរថ្ងៃកំណើត
	Hello.	សួស្ដី
CD2:48	How are you?	សុខសប្បាយទេ?
	I am the music teacher.	ខ្ញុំជាគ្រូបង្រៀនភ្លេង
	Let's sing together.	ចូរច្រៀងជាមួយគ្នា
	My name is _____.	ខ្ញុំឈ្មោះ ____
	Please.	សូម ____
CD2:49	See you next time.	ជួបគ្នាពេលក្រោយ
	Thank you.	អរគុណ
	Try again.	សាកម្ដងទៀត
	Very good.	ល្អណាស់
	You're welcome.	មិនអីទេ

Instructional Phrases	ENGLISH	CANTONESE
CD2:50	Did the melody go up, go down, or stay the same?	那個旋律有高一點，低一點，還是一樣呢？
	Do what I do.	跟著我做。
	Don't talk.	不要講話。
	Echo back.	回音。
CD2:51	Form a line.	排成一條線。
	Form a circle.	排成圓圈。
	Go get _____.	去拿…。
	groups	小組
	Divide into groups.	分成小組
CD2:52	How does this sound?	這個聲音怎麼樣？
	Listen carefully.	聽清楚。
	Look at me.	吞著我。
	Make this sound.	弄這個聲音。
	March in a circle.	在圓圈裡面步行。
CD2:53	partners	伙伴
	Change partners.	交換伙伴。
	Face your partner.	面向你的伙伴。
	Select a partner.	選擇一個伙伴。
	Pick it up.	拾起來。
	Put your hands in your lap.	把你的手放在腿上面。
CD2:54	Raise your hand.	舉起你的手。
	Raise your hand before speaking.	講話之前，要先舉手。
	ready	預備
	Ready, begin.	預備，開始。
	Ready, move.	預備，行。
	Ready, play.	預備，彈。
	Ready, sing.	預備，唱。
CD2:55	Stand side by side.	平排站立。
	This is called _____.	這個叫做…。
	Turn and face me.	轉個來面向我。

McGraw-Hill School Division

Instructional Words

	ENGLISH	CANTONESE
CD2:56	begin	開始
	bow	鞠躬
	clap	拍手
	conduct	指揮
	different	不同
CD2:57	enter	進入
	left hand	左手
	to the left	到左邊
	listen	聆聽
	pat	輕拍
	move	走
CD2:58	read	讀
	return	回來
	right hand	右手
	to the right	到右邊
	say	講
	show me	給我看
CD2:59	sing	唱
	speak	說
	think	想
	wait	等
	whisper	輕輕說
	write	寫

Greetings and Courtesies

CD2:60	Excuse me.	不好意思。
	Goodbye.	再見。
	Good try.	好嘗試。
	Happy birthday!	生日快樂！
	Hello.	你好。
CD2:61	How are you?	你好嗎？
	I am the music teacher.	我是音樂老師。
	Let's sing together.	大家一齊唱。
	My name is _____.	我的名字是…。
	Please.	請。
CD2:62	See you next time.	下次再見。
	Thank you.	謝謝。
	Try again.	再來一次。
	Very good.	非常好。
	You're welcome.	不用客氣。

Instructional Phrases	ENGLISH	HMONG
CD2:63	Did the melody go up, go down, or stay the same?	Zuaj nkauj lub suab mus siab los mus nqis los yog nyob twj ywm qhov qub xwb?
	Do what I do.	Ua li uas kuv ua.
	Don't talk.	Tsi txhob hais lus.
	Echo back.	Hais lawv qab kuv.
CD2:64	Form a line.	Ua ib txoj kab.
	Form a circle.	Ua ib lub vaaj voog.
	Go get _____.	Mus muab_____.
	groups	paab
	Divide into groups.	Ua tej paab.
CD2:65	How does this sound?	Lub suab nov zoo li cas?
	Listen carefully.	Mloog zoo zoo.
	Look at me.	Sai kuv.
	Make this sound.	Ua lub suab nov.
	March in a circle.	Taug kev ua ib lub vaaj voog.
CD2:66	partners	tus khub
	Change partners.	Pauv khub.
	Face your partner.	Saib koj tus khub.
	Select a partner.	Xaiv ib tug khub.
	Pick it up.	Muab khaws.
	Put your hands in your lap.	Muab koj txhais ces tso ntawm koj txhais kaw taws.
CD2:67	Raise your hand.	Tshaa koj txhais ces.
	Raise your hand before speaking.	Tshaa koj txhais ces ua tej koj hais lus.
	ready	npaaj tau lawm los
	Ready, begin.	Npaaj tau lawm ces pib.
	Ready, move.	Npaaj tau lawm ces txaav.
	Ready, play.	Npaaj tau lawm ces ua.
	Ready, sing.	Npaaj tau lawm ces hu nkauj.
CD2:68	This is called _____.	Ntawm nov yog hu ua_____.
	Turn and face me.	Tig los saib kuv.

McGraw-Hill School Division

Instructional Words

	ENGLISH	HMONG
CD2:69	begin	pib
	bow	pe
	conduct	yoj ces
CD2:70	enter	nkag los
	left hand	sab laug
	to the left	mus rau sab laug
	listen	mloog lus
	move	txaav
CD2:71	read	twm ntawd
	return	rov qaab
	right hand	sab xis
	to the right	txav rau sab xis
	say	hais
	show me	qhia kuv
CD2:72	sing	hu nkauj
	speak	hais lus
	think	xav
	whisper	ntxhi

Greetings and Courtesies

CD2:73	Excuse me.	Thov zam kuv.
	Goodbye.	Mus zoo.
	Good try.	Zoo kawg.
	Happy birthday!	Nyob zoo nub yug!
	Hello.	Nyob zoo.
CD2:74	How are you?	Koj nyob li ca lawm os?
	I am the music teacher.	Kuv yog tus naiskhu ua qhia suab nkauj.
	Let's sing together.	Sawvdaws hu nkauj ua ke.
	My name is _____.	Kuv lub npe hu ua_____.
	Please.	Thov.
CD2:75	See you next time.	Sib ntsib dua lawm zag.
	Thank you.	Ua tsaug.
	Try again.	Sim ib zag ntxiv.
	Very good.	Zoo kawg lawm.
	You're welcome.	Tsi ua li ca.

Instructional Phrases	ENGLISH	VIETNAMESE
CD2:76	Did the melody go up, go down, or stay the same?	Âm thanh đi lên, đi xuống hay ở ngang nhau?
	Do what I do.	Hãy làm như tôi.
	Don't talk.	Đừng nói chuyện.
	Echo back.	Lập lại.
CD2:77	Form a line.	Sắp hàng một.
	Form a circle.	Sắp thành vòng tròn.
	Go get _____.	Đi lấy ____.
	groups	nhóm
	Divide into groups.	Chia thành từng nhóm.
CD2:78	How does this sound?	Nghe như thế nào?
	Listen carefully.	Nghe cho kỹ.
	Look at me.	Nhìn tôi đây.
	Make this sound.	Làm như âm thanh nầy.
	March in a circle.	Đi vòng tròn.
CD2:79	partners	cặp bạn
	Change partners.	Đổi bạn.
	Face your partner.	Đối diện bạn mình.
	Select a partner.	Chon ban.
	Pick it up.	Lượm lên.
	Put your hands in your lap.	Để tay kên đùi mình.
CD2:80	Raise your hand.	Giơ tay lên.
	Raise your hand before speaking.	Giơ tay lên trước khi nói.
	ready	sẵn sàng
	Ready, begin.	Sẵn sàng, bắt đầu.
	Ready, move.	Sẵn sàng, đi chuyển.
	Ready, play.	Sẵn sàng, chơi.
	Ready, sing.	Sẵn sàng, hát.
CD2:81	Stand side by side.	Đứng ngang nhau.
	This is called _____.	Cái nầy gọi là ____.
	Turn and face me.	Quay lại đối mặt tôi.

	ENGLISH	VIETNAMESE
CD2:82	begin	*bắt đầu*
	bow	*cúi đầu*
	clap	*vỗ tay*
	conduct	*dẫn*
	different	*khác nhau*
CD2:83	enter	*đi vào*
	left hand	*tay trái*
	to the left	*qua bên trái*
	listen	*nghe*
	pat	*vỗ nhe*
	move	*dời đi*
CD2:84	read	*đoc*
	return	*trở lai*
	right hand	*tay mặt*
	to the right	*qua bên mặt*
	say	*nói*
	show me	*chỉ cho tôi*
CD2:85	sing	*hát*
	speak	*nói*
	think	*suy nghĩ*
	wait	*chờ*
	whisper	*nói thì thào*
	write	*viết*

Greetings and Courtesies

CD2:86	Excuse me.	*Xin lỗi.*
	Goodbye.	*Xin chào.*
	Good try.	*Được lắm.*
	Happy birthday!	*Mừng sinh nhật.*
	Hello.	*Chào.*
CD2:87	How are you?	_____ *mạnh giỏi khong?*
	I am the music teacher.	*Tôi là giáo sư âm nhạc.*
	Let's sing together.	*Cùng hát chung nhau.*
	My name is _____.	*Tên tôi là _____.*
	Please.	*Làm ơn.*
CD2:88	See you next time.	*Gặp nhau lần tới.*
	Thank you.	*Cám ơn.*
	Try again.	*Thử lại đi.*
	Very good.	*Giỏi lắm.*
	You're welcome.	*Không có chi.*

McGraw-Hill School Division

ASIAN CELEBRATIONS CALENDAR

You may refer to this calendar to focus your use of *Share World Music,* choosing materials to go with the date or season for which music is desired. To broaden students' explorations of Asian cultures, consider working with teachers of various subject areas. Offer materials in music class that relate to upcoming areas of study or themes such as a particular season, holiday, or country. In addition, you may wish to coordinate the use of selections from this book with holiday and cultural celebrations in your community.

Date/Time Period	Song	Page	Celebration	Country/Culture
mid-September (8th lunar month)	Tết Trung	52	Tết Trung (Mid-Autumn Festival, Children's Festival)	Vietnam
late October–early November	Diwali Song	66	Diwali (New Year)	India
October–December (during full moon)	Pung Noy Loy Kratong	54	Loy Kratong	Thailand
October–January	Ua Txiab	48	Hmong New Year	Laos, China, Vietnam, and Myanmar (Hmong)
January–February (second new moon of winter)	Bo Hai Huan Ten (listening)	115	Chinese New Year	China
	Chinese Lion Dance (listening)	114	Chinese New Year; also special occasions such as store openings	China
March	Holi Song (listening)	114	Holi (Color Festival)	India
April	Suk San Wan Pi Mai	42	Pi Mai (New Year)	Laos (Buddhist)
first day of spring	Haji Firuz (listening)	115	Noruz (New Year)	Iran
spring	Sakura	34	Cherry Blossom Festival, spring	Japan
May–June (7 weeks after Passover)	Hag Shavuot	32	Shavuot (Festival of First Fruits)	Israel (Jewish)
anytime	Fung Yang Song	60	any celebration	Chinese

SUGGESTED WEB SITES

You may wish to explore these Web sites before or during the study of a particular selection from *Share World Music*. Share your findings with students or assist them in using the sites, as appropriate to the class.

WEB SITES FROM *SHARE WORLD MUSIC* LESSONS

Hag Shavuot (Festival of First Fruits)
To read about the history of Shavuot, visit "Shavuot."
http://www.holidays.net/shavuot/

Kaeru No Uta (Frog's Song)
For pictures and information about frogs, visit "Frogland."
http://www.teleport.com/~dstroy/index.html

San Lun Tsa (Three-Wheeled Taxi)
To see how Chinese characters for numbers are drawn, visit "Animated Chinese Characters."
http://www.ocrat.com/ocrat/chargif/numbers.html

Shiau Ya (Little Duck)
Visit "Sounds of the World's Animals" to explore how people express animal sounds in many languages.
http://www.georgetown.edu/cball/animals/animals.html

Suk San Wan Pi Mai (New Year's Song)
For general background on the people and places of Laos, see "Discovering Laos, The Land of a Million Elephants."
http://www.laoembassy.com/discover/index.htm

ADDITIONAL RELATED WEB SITES

Chang (Elephant)
Visit "Riddle's Elephant and Wildlife Sanctuary" (click on Elephant Biographies).
http://www.hendrix.edu/elephant/frames3.htm

Niam Es, Nim Yog Xyoo Nuav (In This Year), and Ua Txiab
"WWW Hmong Homepage" offers many links to informative sites on Hmong history and culture.
http://www.stolaf.edu/people/cdr/hmong

Pung Noy Loy Kratong (Full Moon Float)
"The Rituals and Traditions of Thai Classical Dance" offers information about classical Thai dance and drama.
http://www.mahidol.ac.th/Thailand/art/dance.html

Tết Trung (Children's Festival)
To learn more about the Vietnamese lantern festival, check the following sites:
• "Sixth Annual Mid-Autumn Festival"
http://www.vietgate.net/midautumn/about/
• "Mid-Autumn Festival, The Children's Festival" (click on Program)
http://www.vietscape.com/events/tt96/index.html
• "Mid-Autumn Festival, The Children's Festival"
http://www.best.com/~vtb/events/tt97/pix0.html

Tang Tang Juen (Round, Round, Turn)
For pictures and more information on traditional dragon boats, visit these sites:
• "Awakening the Dragon"
http://www.ntnu.edu.tw/mtc/dragon.htm
• "Royal Bank Aquafest '97"
http://www.hamilton-went.on.ca/aquafest/dbgenral.htm
• "Cambridge Dragon Boat Club"
http://dialspace.dial.pipex.com/town/terrace/rca79/index.htm
• "Dragon Boat"
http://www.htnu.edu.tw/mtc/dragon.htm

GENERAL RESOURCES

For resources and links of particular interest to music teachers, see these sites:
• "McGraw-Hill School Division Teaching Resources: Music"
http://www.mmhschool.com/teach/music/music1.html
• "McGraw-Hill School Division Music Products"
http://www.mmhschool.com/products/mus3.html

McGraw-Hill School Division

ASIAN RESOURCES IN *SHARE THE MUSIC*

This lists many of the songs, speech pieces, listening selections, literature, and fine art selections from Asian/Asian American, Oceanic, Middle Eastern, and Russian cultures in the *Share the Music* series.

McGraw-Hill School Division

PRONUNCIATION KEY

This Key is an important tool that helps students learn to pronounce diverse languages authentically and with ease.

The International Phonetic Alphabet (IPA) provides pronunciation at the point of use, underlaid beneath song lyrics. IPA was developed in 1888 to facilitate the accurate pronunciation of all languages. Each symbol in IPA represents one sound, so IPA provides one consistent set of symbols for sounds from diverse languages, including non-English sounds that other phonetic systems fail to take into account. The use of simplified IPA limits the number of symbols students encounter, further encouraging ease of use and success.

PRONUNCIATION KEY
SIMPLIFIED INTERNATIONAL PHONETIC ALPHABET

VOWELS

ɑ	f<u>a</u>ther	æ	c<u>a</u>t
e	<u>a</u>pe	ɛ	p<u>e</u>t
i	b<u>ee</u>	ɪ	<u>i</u>t
o	<u>o</u>bey	ɔ	p<u>a</u>w
u	m<u>oo</u>n	ʊ	p<u>u</u>t
ʌ	<u>u</u>p	ə	<u>a</u>go

SPECIAL SOUNDS

β	say *b* without touching lips together; *Spanish* nue<u>v</u>e, ha<u>b</u>a
ç	<u>h</u>ue; *German* i<u>ch</u>
ð	<u>th</u>e, *Spanish* to<u>d</u>o
ɲ	sound <u>n</u> as individual syllable
ö	form [o] with lips and say [e]; *French* ad<u>ieu</u>, *German* sch<u>ö</u>n
œ	form [ɔ] with lips and say [ɛ]; *French* c<u>oeu</u>r, *German* pl<u>ö</u>tzlich
ɾ	flipped r; bu<u>tt</u>er
r̄	rolled r; *Spanish* pe<u>rr</u>o
ǂ	click tongue on the ridge behind teeth; *Zulu* ng<u>c</u>wele
ü	form [u] with lips and say [i]; *French* t<u>u</u>, *German* gr<u>ü</u>n
ü̆	form [ʊ] with lips and say [ɪ]
x	blow strong current of air with back of tongue up; *German* Ba<u>ch</u>, *Hebrew* <u>H</u>anukkah, *Spanish* ba<u>j</u>o
ʒ	plea<u>s</u>ure
'	glottal stop, as in the exclamation "uh oh!" [ˈʌ ˈʔo]
~	nasalized vowel, such as French b<u>on</u> [bõ]
˥	end consonants *k*, *p*, and *t* without puff of air, such as s<u>k</u>y (no puff of air after *k*), as opposed to *kite* (puff of air after *k*)

OTHER CONSONANTS PRONOUNCED SIMILAR TO ENGLISH

ch	<u>ch</u>eese	ny	o<u>ni</u>on, *Spanish* ni<u>ñ</u>o
g	<u>g</u>o	sh	<u>sh</u>ine
ng	si<u>ng</u>	ts	boa<u>ts</u>

ACKNOWLEDGMENTS

Grateful acknowledgment is given to the following authors, composers, and publishers. Every effort has been made to trace the ownership of all copyrighted material and to secure the necessary permissions to reprint these selections. In the case of some selections for which acknowledgment is not given, extensive research has failed to locate the copyright holders.

Hooshang Bagheri for *Haji Firuz*. Copyright © Hooshang Bagheri.

Margaret Campbelle-duGard for *Kaeru No Uta*, collected by Margaret Campbelle-duGard. Copyright © by Margaret Campbelle-duGard.

Miriam B. Factora for *Maliit Na Gagamba* and *Sasara Ang Bulaklak* from MUSICAL FOLK GAMES OF MANILA (PHILIPPINES). Copyright © 1989 by Miriam B. Factora, Manila, Philippines.

Vilay Her for *Ua Txiab; Nim Yog Xyoo Nuav;* and *Niam Es*, collected and transcribed by Vilay Her. Copyright © 1997 by Vilay Her.

Le Van Khoa for *Chuột Cắp Trú'ng*. Copyright © Le Van Khoa.

Kathy B. Sorensen for *Chang; Chuôt Cắp Trú'ng; Deta, Deta; Diwali Song; Hoe Ana Te Vaka; Hong Tsai Me Me; Lek Kansaing; Pung Noy Loy Kratong; San Lun Tsa; Sarika Kaio; Shiau Ya; Suk San Wan Pi Mai; Tết Trung; Tititorea; Tsing Chun U Chü;* and *Wang Ü Ger*, collected and transcribed by Kathy B. Sorensen. Copyright © 1991 by Kathy B. Sorensen.

All singable English translations are owned by McGraw-Hill School Division.

ILLUSTRATION CREDITS

Fian Arroyo, 13; Zina Saunders, 47; Guoliang Wu, 85–86; all others by Duane Gillogly

McGraw-Hill School Division

ALPHABETICAL INDEX OF SONGS AND LISTENINGS

Use this index to locate songs and listenings in *Share World Music* and to find additional lesson plans and ideas in the *Share the Music* Teacher's and Pupil Editions.

*See the appropriate grade level of *Orchestrations for Orff Instruments*.